Seasons and their Festivals

Karl König in the first years of Camphill (early 1940s)

> May the circle of this year
> Every day and every hour
> Be for you a space where peace can live.
> So that from your soul's very depths
> Each heart-beat speaks with great sincerity
> 'Yes'
> To freedom I will offer space.

*Karl König – written as motto on a calendar for 1963
(Translation, Mark and Rosalind Gartner)*

Seasons and their Festivals

Human, Earthly and Cosmic Rhythms

Karl König

Floris Books

Karl König Archive Publication, Vol. 21
Subject: Christianity and Festivals
Edited by Richard Steel

Series editor: Richard Steel

Karl König's collected works are issued by
the Karl König Archive, Aberdeen

First published in English by Floris Books in 2022
© 2022 Trustees of the Karl König Archives

All rights reserved. No part of this publication may
be reproduced without the prior permission of
Floris Books, Edinburgh
www.florisbooks.co.uk

 Also available as an eBook

British Library CIP Data available
ISBN 978-178250-790-1
Printed & bound by MBM Print SCS Ltd, Glasgow

 Floris Books supports sustainable forest management by
printing this book on materials made from wood that
comes from responsible sources and reclaimed material

Contents

Karl König and the Festivals *by Richard Steel*	7
The Human Being and the Festivals of the Year	19
The Human Being and the Cycle of the Year	37
The Year as a Living Being	45
Individual and Historic Conscience	57
A Michaelmas Lecture, 1965	66
An Experience of Music and Destiny, Advent 1954	84
On the Significance of the Twelve Holy Days	91
New Year's Eve Address, 1965–66	99
The 'Entry into Jerusalem'	103
The Experience of Easter Within the Human Being	108
World Breath and World Pulse	114
Human Breath and Human Pulse	127
Easter, the Festival of Resurrection	139
Earthly Creation, Human Form and Human Ego	154
Whit Sunday Address	169
Whitsun Address	178
Notes	191
Bibliography	199
Index	201

Karl König and the Festivals

Richard Steel

Karl König knew quite early in his work as physician and curative educator that the festivals of the year are a crucial area of life for human beings standing between their earthly surroundings below and their heavenly origins above. They are milestones in the development of the individual and of community: the rhythms, the repetition and the experience of inner growth or enrichment being significant nourishment for both. It became his central concern in what was to become his life's work in pioneering the Camphill movement. The first contribution in this volume is also an early lecture, given by König at Whitsun, 1932, in Pilgramshain, in what is now the Polish village Żółkiewka. He had moved there in 1929, married Tilla (née Maasberg) and co-founded the curative home. For Christmas, 1932, the text was translated into English for the journal *Anthroposophy*.

Biographically it was significant that König had such a distinct experience of his own task of destiny in direct connection with a festival. It occurred during his first celebration at the beginning of Advent in the Arlesheim children's home Sonnenhof (also meaning 'Sun Farm').[1] He quickly recognised that the strength of festivals can only be properly developed in social life, in community, and that community building relies on the celebration of festivals. König's connection to the Earth as a living being featured significantly in his move to Silesia, where he co-founded the Pilgramshain community for children with special needs in a landscape that impressed him deeply. It was a landscape that had been nurtured for centuries by the Moravian Brethren, and it was also close to the birthplace of biodynamic agriculture in Koberwitz. The family who offered their castle for his work remained connected over generations with König and what became the Camphill movement. Joachim von Jeetze, the then owner of Pilgramshain Castle, had been present when Rudolf Steiner gave his ground-breaking lectures on agriculture, and he had begun to implement these ideas on his land already in 1924. When König arrived there in 1929 it had become a hub for research into new methods aimed at re-connecting the earth with the cosmos and healing the land through rhythmical processes. It became clear that there was synergy to build on.

Having missed the chance to meet Rudolf Steiner himself, Karl König connected all the more closely with Steiner's assistant and co-developer of anthroposophic medicine and curative education, Ita Wegman. Rudolf Steiner had intended Ita Wegman to also be instrumental in developing the new methods of agriculture, and she carried his intentions for the healing of the human being, the earth and social life with great seriousness. In Karl König, Ita Wegman saw a companion with a similarly strong will to bring these ideals to realisation.

In all these areas rhythm was of vital importance. It became a core field of work for König, and through this work the seasons and their festivals also received a new significance for him. Later on, with the founding of the Camphill movement in Scotland and feeling a greater freedom to unfold his activity, König made the study of the seasons and their festivals a central task.[2]

In connection with König's work for Ita Wegman in

Arlesheim, another festival revealed its significance. He had been tasked with giving a lecture on embryology on the Monday of Whitsun, 1928. König's work in that field had been one reason why Wegman had invited him to Arlesheim, so that he might give courses for physicians and therapists and publish on this subject, which was still a relatively new science then. Although up until that Whitsun König's work and lectures had been well received, he was suddenly and strongly criticised by the leadership of the Anthroposophical Society, which subsequently led to his expulsion in 1935. König felt certain that this sudden change had to do with this particular Whitsun festival, which was exactly 100 years after the appearance of Kaspar Hauser in Nuremberg, on Whitsun Monday in 1828.[3] Whitsun later became a central festival for Camphill, the opening of Kirkton House in Scotland being on Whitsun of 1939,[4] and Kaspar Hauser became not only a theme of study from then on, but like a 'patron saint' for the curative work.

König's intensive inner work with the *Calendar of the Soul*, which he consciously took up in 1933, became another cornerstone of his work and of the community building in Camphill.[5] Towards the end of his life, in what was almost a revelation of his own destiny (he would die the following Easter), König pointed to that year during his address for New Year, 1966:

> It is now 33 years since the beginning of the events in Middle Europe that led to the destruction of Germany and large parts of the world. We will remember that 33 years ago the Beast appeared out of the depths and started to slay everything that wanted to be filled with a certain amount of goodwill. Whoever is not willing to see this must remain blind and dumb for everything that happens

in the world today, because what started in 1933 brought about the chaos in which we have to live now and will still have to live in the years to come. What happened then was meant to veil, to destroy, something else that happened at the same time. To this I still want to refer. You see, the triangle and the melody of Kyrios-Jupiter and that reaching out towards the sign of the Lion, want to remind us and strengthen our belief for the other event that happened in 1933. The being of Christ began to appear within the whole etheric sphere of the Earth.[6]

In the light of this task, which he experienced so deeply, we can see the background to König's healing work. In 1959 he said the following in his annual report to the Camphill movement:

Is the movement identical with curative education only? It is not. Where the image of the human being and of the earth is distorted and humiliated, the movement is going to have its place.[7]

For König, rhythm became an important factor in community life. It linked the healing impulse for human beings and of social life itself with the daily, weekly and seasonal rhythms of the earth, thereby placing these processes in the context of cosmic rhythms. The breathing process of the human being corresponds to the breathing of the earth. The importance of harmonising the human being's breathing processes for healing purposes was deeply rooted in König's anthroposophical medical work, but this was also presented by Rudolf Steiner in the founding of the Waldorf School in 1919 as the fundamental aim in aiding childhood development.[8] It became evident through his later lectures that the development of the human being, as an individual and as a social being, also depends to a great extent on this question of breathing. From early on in the Camphill movement, efforts were made to live in a very practical manner in harmony with the breathing process of the Earth and the cosmos.

In his lecture series on this breathing process, Rudolf Steiner pointed to the enormous context and importance that stands behind these facts:

> People must learn once more to 'think' the spiritual 'together with' the course of nature. It is not admissible today for a person merely to indulge in esoteric speculations; it is necessary today to be able once again to *do the esoteric*. But people will be able to do this only when they can conceive their thoughts so concretely, so livingly that they don't withdraw from everything that is going on around them when they think, but rather that they think with the course of events: 'think together with' the fading of the leaves, with the ripening of the fruits, in a Michaelic way, just as at Easter one knows how to think with the sprouting, springing, blossoming plants and flowers.
>
> When it is understood how to think with the course of the year, then forces will intermingle with the thoughts that will let humanity again hold a dialogue with the divine spiritual powers revealing themselves from the stars. Humanity has drawn down from the stars the power to establish festivals that have an inner human validity. Festivals must be founded out of inner esoteric force. Then from the dialogue with the fading, ripening plants, with the dying Earth, by finding the right inward festival mood, humanity will also again be able to hold converse with the gods and link human existence with divine existence.[9]

This became a deeply held conviction for Karl König, who understood his social endeavours as a space for human development in this direction. Already in 1950 he had written something that serves as an addition to the words quoted above from his report of 1959. They are simple but no less powerful:

> Curative education alone is not our sole purpose, but rather with and through those with special needs to create cultural islands.[10]

'Islands', of course, is not meant here in the sense of segregated communities, but as points of spiritual light within the growing darkness of materialism and the negation of any cosmic connection or responsibilities on the part of humanity. In this sense König was far ahead of his time, pioneering a true form of 'inclusion' based upon those tasks of destiny shared by modern contemporaries.

Social life, as it was to be created through the guidance of Karl König, was to be imbued with beauty and spiritual knowledge. For this reason art always played an important role in community life, finding expression in celebrations that took on many forms. Festivals of any kind are points of culmination, moments of awakening, so to speak, within the rhythmical processes of time. Karl König tasked himself with creating numerous such moments of awakening and recognition – it was said that he would have liked to make every day a festival! At any rate he certainly contributed to deepening the experience of the weekly and yearly rhythms, rather than allowing single festivals to be celebrated in an isolated and abstract manner, or simply out of tradition. Preparation was all important, but so too was the connection of one festival to the next, so that it was possible to experience the standpoint of each day within a whole process.

The plays König wrote for the festivals show his attempt to create threads that lead from one festival to another or, as in the case of the Easter Play, which is written in four parts for each day over Easter, show an inner process leading through the festival.[11] For the ten days between Ascension and Whitsun he wanted to write ten plays marking the inner pathway from one event to the other. In the end, he only managed to finish four of them, but they are a clear statement of his intentions.

In this respect, Karl König expected much from himself and his co-workers. A letter from August, 1961, in which he discusses preparations for the forthcoming Michaelmas festival, shows how seriously he took this participation (see facsimile overleaf).

With the exception of 1955, during which time he was seriously ill, every year from the time of his release from internment on the Isle of Man in 1940, Karl König gave thematic guidance for all festivals. His intention to reach a new level of experience and community participation in the festivals is apparent in the lectures he gave in the early stages of the Camphill movement. It represents a striving for community practice as a path to renewing the festivals in the light of the Michaelic era. Of course, for this the Michael festival itself had a central role. In the lecture he gave on the last Michaelmas festival of his life in 1965, and included in this volume, he said:

> The main question of our times – the central challenge to our whole being – is the struggle for social renewal. And if that does not begin to be found in the course of our times then the necessary renewal of the human being will not be possible. And here I do refer to 'times' and not simply to 'time', because it will be a long process. But this is the task of our times, meaning the time period of Michael. And this needs to come to our awareness right now as we stand at the entrance to the Michaelmas festival.

Dr. Karl König

Camphill House
Milltimber
Aberdeenshire

8. August 1961

Dear ...Alix........,

Michaelmas of this year will be a very important time as the gateway into a period of great and decisive months. The political horizon is darkened and the whole outlook is rather grim. It is our task to turn to the great Powers of Light and to unite with their attempts to lead men and mankind through this present period of darkness.

In this connection I propose that in preparation for Michaelmas we should take up the lectures which Rudolf Steiner held between November 26th and December 22nd 1922. They are published under the title: "Das Verhältnis der Sternenwelt zum Menschen und des Menschen zur Sternenwelt." In these lectures he speaks about the higher self of man; he describes the message of Michael and the being of memory. In relation to the problem of memory I would also advise to study the lecture of March 7th, 1914: "Der Christusimpuls im Zeitwesen und sein Walten im Menschen."

The insight into the meaning of memory and the message of Michael will be our theme during the weeks preceeding Michaelmas.

I hope you will try to walk with many of us in this direction and please make this letter known to your house-community.

With all good wishes
to you and your friends

Yours,

Dr König

Facsimile of letter from Karl König to all those responsible for house communities in Camphill Schools.

This light of Michael was to penetrate the whole of the year, with its festivals as points of consciousness. The Michaelmas festival was to become a community building festival, and König worked tirelessly to enthuse his friends and co-workers to create the content needed. He was a master at initiating such processes, nourishing the community with spiritual science and inspiring cultural activity and the forms to carry them out. Intensive thematic study, artistic practice and socially innovative elements that enriched daily life were woven into the fabric of the growing movement.

The processes that König inaugurated led towards a new experience of time and development – a theme that is to be found in a number of the contributions in this volume. But he also made a sustained effort to link the many lectures he gave over the period of a whole year or sometimes even longer. Almost every year he developed a theme. For instance, he might connect a series of lectures that began on the first Sunday of Advent and lead up to Epiphany or Candlemas (February 2), and he might do the same for Easter. A series of Easter lectures is included in this book; Christmas lectures are planned for a separate volume as they merit a book's worth of discussion in themselves.

Preparation notes for two of König's lectures are also included in this collection, as no other records of the lectures were preserved, but they serve as examples of the way he prepared himself for such events. His diaries and notebooks are full of such preparation, showing the process of his working with a theme. In most of his lectures for the festivals one finds remarks reminding his listeners of the process they were part of. The St John's lecture of 1963 serves as a particular example of his efforts to include the whole community in a thematic process throughout the year. Here he begins by making conscious the various steps they had undertaken together. 'Together' in this case is certainly the correct term, not only because the same group of people were at all the lectures and had heard what he had to say, but also because König had many conversations in between, and lived and worked closely with the communities to make sure that the themes were developed further. Many of those present were able to confirm that, in spite of all his preparation, he let himself be inspired by the mood of the moment, making a strong connection to his audience (this is also apparent by comparison of his preparation notes with the transcripts that were made by note-takers and from recordings). One notices again and again that he spoke of 'our process of festival preparation' or of what 'we' had recognised during a previous festival. This was certainly a real experience for König – as well as for his listeners – and not merely a figure of speech.

In the last years of his life, with his move to Lake Constance and working to build a Middle European Region of Camphill, König prepared festivals in both Scotland and Germany, giving lectures in both locations as well as in many other places on his journeys. For instance, during Advent of 1965, he gave lectures on three Sundays in Föhrenbühl at Lake Constance, and in between them he gave two lectures in Stuttgart on the subject of destiny and an Advent-address in Botton Village on the way to Scotland. Then, after Christmas, from December 29 until Epiphany, he gave four lectures in Scotland under the title of *Body, Soul and Spirit in the Light of Reincarnation and Karma*. In the middle of this series came the last of his New Year's addresses, quoted from above and which is included in this volume. In that year it did not follow the theme of his Christmas lectures, as was otherwise the case, but was quite an independent event, looking to the year ahead in which his own death was to occur. That the theme of the other lectures was destiny seems to be quite an event of destiny in itself!

One can certainly have the impression that König already had a foreboding of his coming death sometime during the Holy Nights of that year, which perhaps led to the lines in the last poem he wrote.[12] This poem grew out of the experience of his last Christmas in Scotland:

> But now the day blusters through the night;
> Lights blind all searching eyes;
> Noises yell into hearkening ears,
> Shrill human speech pierces
> Into the peace-needy heart.
>
> There is the seat of forsaken pain.
> Like a pointing finger it presses
> On the pulse to make it felt,
> Revealing it as existence' source,
> From which our very life wells forth.
>
> Is it an angel's finger?
> Does it herald nearing death?
> Is it a stern indication
> Of an archangel calling you?
>
> Yet quietly the pointing finger
> Calls and says: 'Awaken!'
> 'Awaken', I ask, 'for what?'
> 'Raise your eyes and see above!'
> 'Above', I ask, 'and why?'
> Then I see behind me
> The cloak of Mary, with blue shine,
> Its seams golden rays
> Of the sinking sun of our times.
>
> She carries the child in her hands,
> Wrapped in protecting gesture

In offering towards the pain to come.
I look into the child's countenance
And believe to recognise
Yet know not who it is.

'I am your angel', it tells me,
'Who carries your changing being
Through births and deaths,
Through the wheel of all existence.'

Then the countenance fades
And once more I find myself
In the boisterous light-realm of life.
'Be who you are. Then you
Are true Christmas, yourself.'

Karl König, who gave so much attention to the festivals, was born into Michaelmas (September 25, 1902), made Whitsun and St John's the central motif of his work, had his two significant encounters with his angel during Advent and Christmas (1927 and 1965 respectively) and died during Eastertime in 1966.

The Human Being and the Festivals of the Year

If we consider the Earth in its rhythmic life, we find that its countenance changes as the seasons come and go. A picture of growth and decay, ever arising and passing away, comes before us, and we human beings, for the most part more strongly than we are aware, find ourselves involved in this interplay of the seasons. We live in it and are conditioned by it. We express one mood in the autumn and another in the spring; our being is not the same in summer as it is in winter. Our thoughts, our feelings, even the expressions of our life of will are all influenced by the change of the seasons.

We have only to endeavour to raise these seasonal changes to the level of consciousness and we shall realise their significance and necessity. In the time of winter we become 'homebodies', we want the warmth and comfort of being at home, to be inwardly creative, and to bury ourselves in books and studies and let the world go on as it likes. With the first breath of spring, however, our soul seems to open out again, to take a new interest in the world that is rising up around us. We want to be wanderers, to get to know every corner of the Earth that is changing under the influence of the spring. This feeling intensifies as the forces of spring grow more powerful and summer displays growth and blossom everywhere. We feel then as if we are living in close unity with the life of the Earth: our being seems to have expanded into the very being of the surrounding world, away from our own, personal existence. But with the coming of autumn, interest in our own being revives and we begin to draw back again from the life of the Earth into the realm of personal concerns. Once again we are like hermits who live only for themselves, with hardly a thought for the Earth outside.

Is this not like a great in-breathing and out-breathing in which our being is involved during the course of the seasons? We breathe in our being during autumn in order that we may be our own master in winter, and we breathe it out again in spring in order that we may be one with the Earth in summer.

What is it that is happening in our inner being, leading us out into the world and back again into ourselves? All this is revealed to our sight and, indeed, to all our senses when we contemplate the seasons in their cyclic course. There is a mighty in-breathing and out-breathing in the Earth, too, over the course of the year. The Earth begins to breathe out in the springtime. This out-breathing is complete in the summer and the in-breathing begins again in the autumn. In winter, the Earth returns to herself. The first budding of life in spring, the rising of the sap, the opening of the buds, the unfolding of leaf and blossom are nothing else than the revelations of that mysterious breathing which stirs in the Earth in spring. Higher and higher rises the breath of the Earth-Being, spreading and giving colour to petals, forming the seeds, awakening the animal kingdom to life. Butterflies, beetles, swarming bees: all are permeated by the breath of the Earth as it goes outwards. In summer, the Earth stands still, as it were, with her whole being breathed out. The skies are clear and everything stands at the point of consummation.

When the sun begins to withdraw it draws the breath of the Earth with it. The first leaves begin to fade, the nights are cooler, the clouds of autumn appear on the horizon as a foreboding of the coming winter. The more the leaves fade, the more the ripened fruits fall to the ground, the more the Earth breathes herself in until, in winter, she rests within her own being. Universe and Earth seem to have separated from one another. Never do the starry heavens appear so remote as in winter, and never does the Earth seem so crusted and hard. The colours have vanished, the trees are bare, and white snow lies over the land. This in-breathing and out-breathing of the Earth-Soul, which pulses yearly through the Earth, bears us along with it. It leads us in winter back to our own 'house' and lets our being stream out in summer on the waves of the great process of world-becoming.

We should never be able to comprehend the Earth in her wholeness if we could not experience the seasons that are part of her. The recurring seasonal changes to which the face of Nature is subject are but the expression of the rhythmic beat of time in which the Earth lives. The Earth can only be a complete being in the span of one year. Just as we human beings have head, breast and limbs as members of our body, so the Earth has her spring, summer, autumn and winter, but with this difference: these members of the Earth-Being do not lie beside one another in space but reveal themselves one after each other in time. The body of the Earth is an organism in time; the human body is a structure in space. But the Earth is also membered in her spatial form, as we can see if we pass from north to south. The poles are her winter times, the temperate zones her spatial spring and autumn, and the equatorial region is her permanent summer. And so on the one hand we find that the Earth has her 'seasons in space' and on the other her 'seasons in time'.

If we now realise that we have practically lost sight of the way in which our life is bound up with the seasons, we shall see why it is that we can no longer recognise the power and necessity of the great festivals of the year. Those, however, who live with children soon become aware that these seasonal festivals are necessities of life for the child without which they can hardly exist. The child measures the course of the year almost entirely according to the festivals. They live from one Christmas to the next with Easter in between. It is really an offence against the being of the child to deprive them of any real experience of these festivals and thus to let them grow up as foolish as we ourselves are in this respect. If we no longer believe that these festivals are essential for our own being, we shall naturally find it impossible to accept the idea that they are also essential for the life of the Earth. We have learned to think biologically in the last decades, but we have altogether forgotten to consider soul and spirit.

We think of the Earth merely as a living panorama of growth and decay and have forgotten that above all the waxing and waning life, a power of soul and spirit is at work that nowhere expresses itself so strongly as at the festival times. If these festivals were abolished (as many in this age seem to desire), then not only the human being but the Earth too would be shaken out of the true rhythm of being and lose the forces implicit in the process of breathing.

The festivals are memorial stones of primordial necessities whose nature was changed by what came to pass at the beginning of our era. Just as we human beings have within us our physiological functions, so the Earth has the cyclic events of the seasons. As beings of soul and spirit we are able to work because of these physiological functions, and by keeping them under control we are able to unfold our powers of thinking, feeling and willing. In the same way, through the influence of the soul and spirit of the Earth, the festivals are placed in the seasons as necessities of Earth existence. They are, as it were, spiritual senses of the Earth. Like our own inner experiences, they are the expression of the soul and spirit of the whole planet.

Certainly, from the standpoint of physical science today, the festivals cannot be viewed as earthly necessities in this sense. We must learn to look upon the necessities of the soul and spirit of the Earth in a new light before we shall be able to perceive the origin of the festivals in the union of the Earth-Spirit with the Earth-Body. Just as we ourselves live as beings of soul and spirit in the 'house' of our body, and thought arises at the point where we make contact with our head, feeling at the point of contact with our rhythmic organisation, and willing at the point of contact with our metabolic-limb system; so in the Earth the festivals are born from the meeting of the Earth-Spirit and Earth-Soul with the body of the Earth during the seasons, in the yearly out-breathing and in-breathing. In the spring we have the Easter festival, in summer the festival of St John, in autumn the festival of Michael and in winter the festival of Christmas.

If, in the light of what we have been taught by Rudolf Steiner, we look back to earlier periods of human evolution, we find, for example in ancient Greece, that knowledge and realisation of these things still existed.[1] Not only the individual, but also the people of whole districts experienced the seasons and their festivals as spiritual necessities. According to their varied beliefs they poured into the temples at every season and there they experienced the power going out from the festivals. They came to the temples and the sanctuaries of initiation and there they received the words of wisdom that enabled them to hold their own against the living forces of the seasons. For in those days, too, it was necessary for people not to allow their being to be swallowed up in the flood of Nature processes, but to find a way of raising the soul and spirit above the workings of Nature. Words of guidance were given in the sanctuaries of the mysteries, indicating the means whereby the human soul and spirit might hold their own within the flow of seasonal forces.

In a lecture on the festivals, Rudolf Steiner has told us that in spring and in autumn, in summer and in winter, different commands were given to people as guidance for their conduct and which needed to live in them through the course of the year. Thus in spring the call was:

'Know Thyself!'

During the season when the human soul tends to sink into the flood of the uprising forces of spring, their attention was directed back again to their own being in order that they might not entirely succumb to the Earth. In summer the command was:

'Receive the Light!'

The soul must not be given up passively and blindly to world happenings but, while living in them, consciously receive the streaming light. In the autumn, when the urge of the soul is again to return to its own inner life, the command was:

'Look around Thee!'

Ignore not the world for the sake of thine own being but be awake to all that is happening around thee! And, in winter, when the Earth has completed her in-breathing and the human being is so thrown back upon themselves that they are threatened with inner contraction and immobility, then from the mysteries there came the command:

'Protect Thyself from the Evil!'

The guidance given to human beings in those ancient

times through the word of the gods now expresses itself in the Earth in the festivals. When the gods silenced their voices and no longer entrusted their words of healing and strength to human souls through the mouths of the priests, the Christian festivals entered into the cycle of earthly time. Whoever is able inwardly to experience the Christmas festival protects themselves from the Evil; whoever truly experiences the festival of Easter knows their own being; whoever truly experiences the festival of St John receives the light; and whoever remains awake at the season of Michaelmas and looks around them is attentive to the world. The gods no longer speak through the mouths of priests, but through the festivals, through the soul of each individual. Humanity no longer needs to wander in the world of space to the places of the mysteries in order to receive guidance. In the sense of all that has been revealed by Rudolf Steiner in anthroposophy, humanity has only to ripen to the point of being able to truly experience the festivals of the year. The temples no longer need to be sought in the world of space; they are to be found in the world of time, in the time-cycle of the festivals.

The festivals are also necessary in order that it may be possible for the human soul to rise above the purely biological activities of the body; the festivals contain healing forces that can modify or ennoble the exuberance of life. Those who know what the festivals really are find a pathway to the healing forces of the world that are discovered in spiritual attainment. The forces of the Earth-Spirit, weaving through the festivals, must help us amid the chaos of the modern world to find our true humanity.

Having made this attempt to understand the festivals of the year, as it were, more from the periphery, we will now take a further step by looking not from the periphery towards the centre but from the centre towards the periphery. The human body, as microcosm, bears within itself everything that is spread out in space and time in the surrounding world. The festivals, too, must therefore be sought and found in our bodily organisation. Just as in the world outside the festivals are placed in the seasons, so must they be stamped on the inner being of the human microcosm, in spatial structures that correspond with the seasons.

If we examine the human body in its well-nigh infinite complexity and try to find forms that correspond with the seasons of the year, we must look for structures or organic systems. For just as in the world the four seasons follow one another in the time-body of the earth, so there must be present within the human body four organic structures which, as spatial forms, permeate the whole body. These organic structures will obviously not be single organs but, rather, organic systems that work throughout the human body. If we ask ourselves what these can be, we find four, closely interconnected organic systems, namely bones, muscles, nerves and blood vessels. Each of these four 'organisations' is to be found, in some form, practically everywhere in the human body, above in the head, below in the limbs, in the breast and in the metabolic region, both singly and together. They are, after all, individual structures, just as there are individual muscles, bones, nerve-fibres and blood vessels, but they combine to form the skeleton, the muscular system, the nervous system and the system of blood vessels. Independent of one another as they appear to be, their mutual connections are exceedingly intimate. As in the world outside periods of transition connect spring with summer and autumn with winter, so too, within our body, definite tissues link blood vessels to bones, muscles to nerves, nerves to bones.

But this must not be taken merely as a generalisation. We must seek to understand the whole picture of the organism in its relation to the four seasons of the year. The picture of the blood itself, that very special fluid, will lead us over from one system to the other. As the Earth changes its countenance during the course of the year, from spring through summer and autumn into winter, so does the blood pass from bone to muscle and from muscle to nerve to find its true being within the system of the blood vessels.

Think of the skeleton. It is the hardest structure in our body. The bones lie within the rest of our organism as if they were frozen stiff, and by their very rigidity they hold everything else around them. We think of the bones as inwardly hard, inwardly steeled, full of solid salt deposits. And if we walk over the frozen earth of winter, covered with the crystal forms of snow, we have the impression that this hard, snow-covered earth corresponds in the course of the year to what the skeleton represents in the body. Just as the skeleton is hard and frozen, so is the earth in the time of deep winter. Just as the skeleton is impregnated with salts, so is the earth covered with snow-crystals. In the human body and the body of the Earth, bones and winter correspond.

But this thought can be deepened still further if we reflect that within the hard-shelled bones there are many delicate, living substances. Within the bones there is the marrow – the perpetual wellspring of the red blood flowing through our bodies. It is here that the red blood corpuscles germinate unceasingly, in order ever and again to restore the older blood and to serve as the means for the renewal of bodily substance. In like manner do the seeds of the coming spring germinate beneath the hard, frost-bound earth in winter. It is there that millions of seeds are forming, to appear as green plants when at the first breaking of spring the earth thrusts them upwards. Just as the colourless marrow-cells are transformed into red blood when they have passed through the bones, so are the colourless seed-germs beneath the hard crust of the earth in winter transformed into the green veil of plant life in spring. Bones and the Earth in winter – both bear within their hardened shells the wellspring of life.

But if we pass over the Earth in spring in the mood of the wanderer that comes upon us in this season, if we encounter the constant interplay of diverse forces and then look back into our own being, what do we find within ourselves that corresponds with this outer picture? Gazing at the growing plants, at the interplay of expanding and contracting forces at work in every leaf, bud and blossom, in every plant with its green sap rising and falling with the rhythm of day and night, then we find an organic system within us corresponding with this picture of the earth in spring: our muscular system. Just as the pulsing stream of blood pours through our muscles, giving them the power of contraction and expansion that enables our body to move, so does the rising and falling sap stream through the growing plants in outer nature. Our muscular structure is red and full of life. Fibre by fibre the muscles are threaded together, just as fibre by fibre stem and leaf take shape in the green plant. The bones constitute the firm, solid region of our body; the muscles are permeated through and through with fluids and are, as a matter of fact, simply thickened fluid substance. Their shapes are not rigid and clear-cut but involved in perpetual change. The ebb and flow in the earth is expressed in the muscles through their contraction and expansion. What expresses itself in the rising and falling sap of springtime is, in the muscles, the pulsing stream of blood and the consequent contraction and expansion of muscular tissue. The muscles, in short, represent the springtime of the human body. The blood is not actually formed in the muscle as it is in the bones, but in the muscle the blood unfolds its own active forces. Thus does the earth in spring express its own youthful life, bearing it onwards into the period of summer.

And now let us think of summer. The out-breathing of

the Earth is at its climax. The Earth abounds with the forces whereby fruits and flowers are ripened. Just as in winter it is the Earth herself that provides the characteristic picture of the season, and in spring the green plant covering, so now, in summer, it is the world of flower and fruit. Colours in all their variety cover the Earth with glory, replacing the green of spring. The Earth seems to have reached the highest point of outer completion and is now at rest, waiting as it were until the time of her in-breathing. Midsummer is a time of standstill in the highest sense. Just as we may pause in a long outward breath when we have given ourselves over entirely to some outer impression, so does the Earth in summer pause, although reminded now and then of the coming autumn by thunder, lightning and stormy weather.

In the human body, too, there is a system that has reached the highest point of completion, namely, the nervous system. The nerves lie finished and complete in our body, not hard like the bones nor alive like the muscles. Like summer, the nerves represent the highest development of the forces of life-activity within our being. The nerves are the personification within us of a perpetual summertime and if we contemplate them with living vision they seem to stream out like a sun shining always at highest strength, spreading light and burning warmth which, when they become too powerful (as sometimes happens in summer) works destructively. Just as in summer nothing is capable of further change, so also in the nerves is everything finished. The upbuilding process in the nerves is complete; they are capable of no further development and now can only be subject to the forces of demolition. The nerves are polar to the blood. In the nerves the blood has no free passage of its own; it is overpowered. Just as in summer the Earth has lost her own being and is given over in a state of passivity to the in-working forces of cosmic space, so too is the blood overwhelmed in the nerves. In blossom and fruit, the sap flowing in the greenness of plant life is purified, raised to a higher level of being. The forces expressed in flower and fruit are not of earthly origin; the forces of the stars have here come down to earth. In summer the heavens have descended and dominate the Earth, just as in our body the nerves restrain the life of the blood, subdue it and assert their own being.

But just as the thunderstorms of summer augur the approach of autumn, which dampens down the exuberance of life with a spiritual force and brings in its train shortening days, clear air and driving clouds, so the blood system confronts the nerves in order to rid them of their superabundant activity and to warn them of their passing. Just as the blood within us can only create irreparable injury if it breaks through the wall dividing it from the nerve tissue, so does the autumn break into summer, disturbing its repose. Autumn checks the exuberant life, leads it back again to the earth, teaches it how to find the soil again. The blood vessels are an image of autumn within us. They bear the forces of the flowing blood through the body, they tint the organs just as autumn tints the leaves, and the blood within them is involved in a constant process of demolition, akin to the processes of autumn. The blood within us draws the stream of breathed-in air into the body, just as the autumn directs the earth breath back to the soil. If we have characterised the bones as hard, the muscles as living, and the nerves as finished and complete, then we must regard the blood as an element containing inner fire, but one steeled and purified by forces we have yet to discover.

As the period of autumn connects the phase of the greatest outpouring of the Earth with the phase of deepest descent in winter, so too it is the system of blood vessels in us that unites the above and the below, participating in the upbuilding processes yet at the same time bearing forces of destruction. Circulation holds the blood within coordinated paths, just as the autumnal Earth draws her life back to herself again. What is represented by the dark, catabolic venous system and the bright, anabolic arterial system is, in the muscles, contraction and expansion. Spring and autumn are the intermediaries between winter and summer; the muscles and the blood vessels are likewise intermediaries between bones and the nerves. In winter and in summer the world stands still; in bones and nerves the process of organic formation has come to rest. Through the blood vessels and the muscular system this process is involved in the constant ebb and flow of constructive and destructive activity, just as spring and autumn are the intermediaries between the conditions of stillness prevailing in summer and winter.

Now that we have discovered the seasons within the human body – winter in the bones, spring in the muscles, summer in the nerves, autumn in the blood vessels – we can venture one step further and ask: are the festivals connected with these seasons also to be found in an organic form within the body? All the systems we have described, and which may be thought of as the seasons within the human body, would be incomplete if each did not possess a central organ. Just as the seasons of the year would be incomplete without the festivals, so too, within our body, there are four organic structures buried mysteriously within the systems of bones, muscles, nerves and blood vessels.

If we study the bone system taken as a whole with skull, ribs, limbs and spinal column, we find it to be a firmly united, harmoniously formed structure. It is complete in itself, a perfectly self-enclosed structure. But it would be condemned to destruction if there were not living within it, like a seed, something whereby its future is assured. In the time of deepest winter, when the Earth has breathed in and is enclosed within her own being, the inner light of Christmas begins to shine. Out of this light the hope of re-awakening glimmers in its first rays. Likewise embedded within the bone system, not belonging to it and yet its noblest part, lies the larynx. It is the cradle in which the word is perpetually born, even as at Christmas the Light of the World was born. Without a larynx the bones would lose their purpose; without Christmas the earth would ossify. In the season of winter lies the feast of the birth of Christ. Within the skeleton lies the larynx, the organ which gives birth to our words.

Easter falls in the season of spring. Easter points us to the central point of the whole sweep of human history, to the event that Rudolf Steiner always referred to as the Mystery of Golgotha. Within our muscular system too there lies an organ that may justly be called the central point of our whole being, namely the heart. It is itself a muscle, the constant preserver and sustainer of our existence. Everything radiates from it and back to it again. All the muscles are grouped around the heart, receiving from there the stream of blood and sending the blood back to the heart again. The heart is the permanent centre of our being, just as the Easter festival is the eternal centre of the whole evolutionary process of the Earth and of humanity. Renewing forces, forces that are wellsprings of life, stream out from Easter to human souls and back again. This festival of spring is the festival of the conquest over death, which our heart, in its perpetual beating, celebrates unceasingly. The heart is the most central muscle, the bestower of life through the power of the overcoming of death, which it bears within itself.

As the larynx redeems the hardening of the bone system and thus becomes the fulfiller of the command, 'Protect Thyself from the Evil', so is the heart, because it is the wellspring of life, the fulfiller of the command 'Know Thyself'. The great process to which Goethe referred as 'dying and becoming' is expressed as world fact in the Easter festival. It lives as bodily fact perpetually in the heart and works as an act of knowledge in the saying 'Know Thyself'.

The forces of the nerves too would ebb away if there did not lie within the system a small, calcified structure that serves as its centre and which alone makes it possible for human beings to fulfil the command, 'Receive the Light'. The pineal gland, embedded within the brain, is the organ that we may think of as representing the 'festival' in the nervous system. It contains chalk deposits in their most delicate form and, considered with true insight, it is as if this organ represents a kind of counterpart of the bones within the nervous system, as if it had carried the substance of winter into the substance of summer, thus checking the possibility of over-exuberance and beginning the work of demolishing and quelling pride. It is the pineal gland that enables us to 'receive the light' and by inner transformation to awaken to new possibilities of existence. It represents the festival of St John within the body. When, as a reflection of earlier festivals, we light the fires on mountain heights at this midsummer festival and send the flames of the burning wood out into the surrounding world, this is like the clear fire of knowledge shining out from the region of the pineal gland into the spaces of the head. That which in the outer world has solidified into wood and is thus able to burn and glow has densified into the calcified pineal gland from which an inner fire glows continually.

Thus we find the festivals of Christmas, Easter and St John represented within our body, and we can see from this that the festivals are necessities in themselves, just as the larynx, heart and pineal gland are necessities for our existence.

Finally, in autumn, the festival of Michaelmas calls us to alert consciousness, with the command 'Look around Thee'. And now we must try to discover the 'festival' in the system of blood vessels. In a wonderful lecture that he gave on October 5, 1923, Rudolf Steiner indicated how during the season of autumn a picture of what is at work outside in the cosmos can be found in the blood.[2] He spoke of the wonderful meteoric showers that appear at the beginning of autumn, piercing their way through the summer nights, and indicated that we find the corresponding phenomenon in the iron contained within the blood vessels. Just as organic iron is continually precipitated in the red blood corpuscles, and this is the only metal of which any considerable amount is traceable in our body, so do the meteors stream into the autumn atmosphere as the bearers of the spiritual forces that check the exuberant summer and give to the Earth the substance necessary for her in-breathing. By way of the meteors a spiritual power streams into the Earth, a power that destroys life: thus did Rudolf Steiner describe it. We know that it is the iron in the blood that promotes the in-breathing, that draws the oxygen of the air to itself. And it is precisely in the blood vessels that this power of the iron manifests. The meteors in the heavens outside and the iron within us are identical structures.

But in the Michaelmas festival we pay homage to that spiritual power which thrusts the meteors down to the Earth in order to quench the rising vapours of an all too exuberant life. In the picture of Michael and his fight with the dragon we have the same motif. But these forces of the Michael festival live also in the iron within our blood, which continually holds in check the excessive activity of life as it tries to permeate the blood. This makes it possible for the human being to fulfil the command 'Look around Thee'. Because the power of the iron is working, we need not let ourselves sink into the flowing substances of the body but can rise above it and receive the spiritual forces streaming towards us from the being of the Archangel Michael. As with the outer world the dragon of summer is held in check by the meteoric forces of autumn, so too does the iron in the blood keep watch over the dragon who spreads his being over the region of the blood vessels. Thus we are enabled to behold the world and through the world to know ourselves.

And so we have discovered the four festivals of the year in our own body and have been able thereby to realise the sense in which these festivals are necessities. They have not been instituted out of an arbitrary will, nor are they merely the outcome of ancient tradition. They are unconditional necessities of the whole course of nature in which they are placed and to which they belong. Another picture, too, will bring home to us the nature of the festivals still more clearly. Just as humanity stands within the kingdoms of nature, surrounded by but rising above the animal, plant and mineral, so is the festival placed in its season but stands over and above it. A materialistic science believes the human being to be the final product and offspring of the whole organic and inorganic world. The spiritual science of Rudolf Steiner has taught us, however, that mineral, plant and animal could not have come into being had the human being not existed. Mineral, plant and animal have sprung from the human being, not the human being from them.

Similarly, the festivals are the highlights in the course of the yearly seasons. But for that very reason they are the primary impulses around which the seasons have grouped themselves. They stand within the coursing flow of natural life just as the human being stands within the kingdoms of nature. And just as the human being is the bearer of the spirit, the being through whose humanity animal, plant and stone will gradually be redeemed – so are the festivals the bearers of the spirit within the earthly seasons. They are the points at which the Earth-Spirit and the World-Spirit meet. If the human soul can form a new union with these pivotal points of the year, then it can share in the streaming spirit that pours down into the earthly world through the festivals. Humanity and humanity alone can bring healing and redemption into the world of nature.

In like manner do the festivals bring healing and redemption into the course of the year. Through humanity and the festivals, forces of healing pour into the earthly world, and if we unite our being with the festivals, the healing forces will be able to work with their inherent power. Such a union brings the human soul to that Being by whom the festivals have been stamped into the very life of the earth, to that Being of whom it is said: 'In the beginning was the Word.' By the Word all things were made. From the Word streams the power of the four seasons and the four festivals. But from the Word, too, there flows the form of the human body in which the seasons and the festivals have their expression. The innermost essence of the Word is the Healer of the world, the Bearer of the healing forces with which we must work if we are truly to be redeemers. If the human soul receives the powers of Christ into itself, then it can find access to the world of the healing forces and bring these forces into the world. The festivals of the year are a picture of this; the human body, too, is a picture of it. Let us learn once again in full consciousness to truly celebrate the festivals in order that along the path opened up for us by Rudolf Steiner we may draw near to the Christ. In this way we must endeavour to unfold a conscious understanding of the healing forces that are working in the world.

The Human Being and the Cycle of the Year

Anyone whose eyes and heart are even a little open to what is happening around us will notice that we human beings are still deeply rooted in the cycle of the year. We have only to look outside and observe the changes in winter and spring that take place in the plant realm, for example, when it moves from germinating to growing, and then turn that same gaze inward. Then we see how we ourselves have transformative soul experiences as the plants develop. Who doesn't like to sit in a warm living room in winter, reading a book or indulging in pondering world affairs? Similarly, we can feel how when nature awakens, the human soul experiences the urge to turn outward and respond to all the growing and sprouting plants. All human beings become wanderers in the spring, so that we can go anywhere we might see the awakening of nature with our own eyes. When summer draws near, our human soul life wants to bloom along with each blossom, ripen with every fruit. Our gaze is drawn more to the heavens than to the Earth, and we feel as if we are living more in light and warmth than in the limitations and weight of the Earth. And then, when the first autumn storms come, we feel how we begin to draw inward and look forward to returning home to sit quietly, away from the world.

Though we seldom contemplate these feelings today, they nevertheless permeate us deeply. And we can keep this image of the human soul in the cycle of the year before us: in the winter, it is drawn deeply into the nature of the body; in the spring, it opens and begins to wander; in summer, it expands over the Earth; and in the autumn, it returns to itself.

We know from Rudolf Steiner that the cycle of the seasons takes place in a similar way on the Earth. The Earth's soul rests within the Earth in winter, helping plant seeds to develop, and protecting all that is beginning to form within it. The Earth's soul awakens in the spring and strives toward the heavens, then expands to surround the Earth in summer, and finally returns in the autumn, so that it can prepare for the new year in the winter. Rudolf Steiner calls this cycle of the year a great inhalation and exhalation. Our normal human breathing is similar to how the Earth begins to exhale in the spring, has fully exhaled in the summer, and inhales in the autumn so that it can be still in the winter. But the Earth breathes its soul in and out through the cycle of the year, and we can only understand this becoming and dying away if we are truly able to see the Earth's soul as the Earth's breathing. In spring, the Earth's soul grows along with every blade of grass, unfurls with every leaf, and unfolds with every blossom. In summer, the Earth's soul is spread out in all the colourful play of the plant realm. And in the autumn, the last flash of this soul world announces itself in the turning, dying leaves. It is an inner event that shows itself to us in the living cycle of the year. And we humans, as ensouled beings, experience this revelation as if in miniature. It is for this reason that the ancients used the name Persephone both for nature and for the human soul. They were still able to feel how the same forces – the appearance of Persephone from the depths of the Earth and her return to her dark consort, Pluto – are working in both places.

This becoming and dying away is not only an ascent from

and then a descent back into the same substance. It is also, from a broader perspective, a perpetual metamorphosis. The earthly seasons are not coincidences; they are living laws that vary before our eyes in the processes of arising and dying away. If we cannot sense the winter as the seed of the year, and the seasons that develop out of it as the plants that grow from this seed, we will never comprehend the seasons. For winter itself does not only carry and activate the seeds. It is also, in its whole being, a seed from which the 'seasons-plant' originates. We can see how the winter earth itself lies embedded in the cycle of the seasons like a seed: how the high, starry skies are its womb and how this seed begins to germinate in this starry womb as spring nears; how light and warmth begin to flood down in the spring, awakening the seed and forming the leaves and stem of the living plant; how the rain cultivates it, and the thawing air forms it. The being of spring always contains a giving and receiving, which is expressed in the breathing of the leaves. When summer comes, it itself appears to be a blossom, alive in radiating and spreading fragrance. And just as the fruits begin to ripen in the autumn, this season, itself, is a fruit, abundant and full, from whose interior the seed of the new winter emerges.

But if we recognise the seasons as a plant whose fourfoldness contains the whole life of the year – the seed in winter, the leaves in spring, the blossom in summer and the fruit in autumn – the passage of seasons comes alive for us. These seasons are themselves active and creative life, simultaneously carrying within them the form of what they create. Themselves a mighty plant, they perhaps even create the *Urpflanze*, or archetypal plant – the entire plant life of the earth.

And all of the life that is becoming within this 'seasons-plant' carries within it the fourfoldness that is active within it. This fourfoldness occurs in human nature, in the whole of the Earth, in the minerals, animals and plants, and also in true art.

Below, we will attempt to demonstrate this fourfoldness of the cycle of the seasons as it relates to a specific part of human life: the living, constructive forces that we carry within our organism and that find their expression in the circulation of the blood that passes through four particular organs.

Let us look first at the lungs. They lie embedded in our thoracic cavity and support our immediate respiration. In form, they can be compared to a tree, with numerous branches and twigs into which the breath flows and from which it is then released. If we look at the moment of inhalation, in which we have drawn in the air, this is the moment that corresponds to winter in the great breath of the annual cycle. That is when the Earth has breathed in, just as we have breathed in when our lungs are expanded and there is a moment of stillness. But in this moment, a very specific, miraculous occurrence is taking place within us: the living forces in the oxygen that are delivered to us from our environment in the air we inhale combine with the blood that flows through the lungs and re-enliven it. We can see this same process in the cycle of the seasons when the soul of the Earth, which has withdrawn into the Earth, quickens the dormant seeds to new becoming. Just as the Earth's soul approaches each individual plant seed in winter and awakens it to new life, the inhaled air in our lungs approaches each individual blood corpuscle and gives it the life forces it carries with it in the oxygen. This is a more internal process within the lungs, with which, if we pursue it further, another polarity is associated. For as the oxygen with its vital growth forces is taken up by the blood, the blood gives off something else: carbon dioxide. The characteristic process of carbon is fundamental to this.

Rudolf Steiner has taught us that only a portion of the carbon dioxide is expelled with the exhalation of breath.

The other portion strives upwards to the head, from where it determines all of the formative processes that take place in the human organism. Everything within us that is formed – be it our bones, our nerves, the demarcation of our organs or any other form – is founded on the carbon dioxide process. And we can sense how the internal enlivening process takes place within the lungs while, at the same time, an outward formative process is active, which strives to bring everything into a constrained and rigid form. In the same way, the gentle, enlivening force affects the young seeds within the winter earth, while the formative power of wintertime works externally, hardening the earth, forming snow crystals, and bringing rigidity and death into the world. This is the mark of winter – that within the freezing cold, germinating life lies hidden. In the lung process, we find the same thing.

If we continue to follow the internal process of oxygen absorption on its path through the human organism, we come to a second organ: the liver. It has a different form than the lungs. It is not hollow, but rather completely filled with the stream of fluid; a living form, heavy and large. It is the organ in which the absorbed oxygen is given up by the blood and is used to build up fourfold substantiality. The liver is the great chemist within us. Whether it is forming sugars, fats, or proteins, it always takes the living oxygen from the blood and transfers it into substance. It is continuously building, immediately releasing all of the material it has formed into the rest of the organism. It carries within it the secret of the formation of material. It forms complex materials from simple substances; it creates living, working substantiality from simple forms, and floods our organism with these life-giving gifts. It is like the Earth's spring, the great chemist of the cycle of the year. It takes the enlivened seed and forms it into stem and leaf. It gives the leaf the ability to create complex structures from simple substances. It is full of living strength that is constantly taking shape and transforming.

If we look closely, this outward liver process is mirrored by a more inward one. The liver does not only take up living oxygen in order to form new substances; there is a second process working within it. From the many paths that the blood takes within the human organism, it carries nitrogen to the liver, bringing a new element into the circulation. If the oxygen brings life, the nitrogen works in a different way. It does not continuously build the same forms, but rather takes what has already been formed and quietly reshapes it. It restrains life, taking its strength and giving it more form. The same process that causes the metamorphosis of leaf to blossom in the plant is the transition from the oxygen process to the nitrogen process in the human organism. It takes place internally in the liver. What appears here as bile production is an image of this process. And just as the all-too-rich life of the greening plant realm in the spring gradually metamorphoses into the fragrant and colourful multiplicity of blossoms, the internally active nitrogen process in the liver constantly transforms the outwardly striving formative forces of the oxygen.

If we follow this internally oriented liver process further, it leads us to the kidneys, where it becomes an externally oriented process. All the uric acid, urea and substances containing nitrogen that are produced in it have become a process of decay. Only one process in the cycle of the seasons is comparable: the wilting of blossoms. The inwardly active nitrogen process in the liver constantly gives new bloom to our organism and this bloom is constantly wilting in the kidney process. Just as the blaze of a hot summer has a destructive effect on tender blossoms, causing them to wither and bringing forth something new out of their process of decay, all of the blaze of the lower human being surges continuously against the kidneys and causes the nitrogen process in it to wither into the ashes of urine salts. But just as the fruit arises from the dying blossoms, a new process arises within the kidneys, which also has a new element as the basis of its activity: hydrogen. It begins its first, germ-like life there below, becoming stronger and stronger and striving upward. And if we follow it, it leads us up to the heart. There it finds its true home, from which it can pour radiantly into all parts of the body. For the hydrogen process, bringing spiritual forces, spreads out in every direction from the heart, through the blood. It is the true enlivener of all muscle activity, all abundance of work. But as it flows, something new occurs in the empty space that is left behind: the formative forces of carbon. They come into being wherever this outward-flowing activity leaves behind empty space. Finally, we have before us the image of the mature fruit, which carries within it the seeds of a new plant. This is also an image of autumn. It radiates in the colours of the leaves that announce it, working outward spiritually into the cosmos. And in the empty space that is left behind by this radiation, the seed of winter is formed.

From the heart we return to the lungs and rediscover the carbon process. But now it is outward-oriented, and we encounter the new life of oxygen, completing the loop of circulation. We have followed an internal life and activity process of the human being, and we were able to do this because we had the imprint of the seasons as a guide. If we summarise this whole process again, we find the following:

- The internal process of oxygen absorption, facilitated by the lungs.
- The same process in the liver, oriented outwards, and the nitrogen process that comes towards it. In nature, the metamorphosis of plants from leaves to blossom.

- The nitrogen process in the kidneys that turns outward, while the hydrogen process forms internally. In nature, the withering of the blossoms and the beginnings of fruit formation.
- The outward-striving forces of the hydrogen in the heart, analogous in nature to fruit formation, and, at the very centre, the tender becoming of carbon as the seed within the fruit.
- The seed takes on enlivening forces in the lungs, and its shape has a formative effect on everything that exists.

Here again we encounter plant development. We were able to comprehend the 'seasons-plant'. It works continuously within our being in the fourfoldness of the formative forces that we just delineated. As soul-spiritual beings, we are closely connected with these forces. The soul-building forces of the seasons that live within us work as life-building forces, and the two meet each other. And where the two meet, what we are accustomed to call the character of the human being forms. Our affinity to winter or spring, summer or autumn often determines our entire destiny. However, as cognisant human beings, we should not leave it at that. If we grasp the life of the whole year as a totality, our destiny will also become as broad as the Earth, so that we may take the totality of the seasons-plant into our existence and, in this way, experience ourselves in our connection to the entire Earth.

The Year as a Living Being

Lecture in Camphill Hall, June 23, 1963

Dear friends

The eve of St John's day has arrived, and with this time the ever-occurring question: is it altogether justified for us – being Christians – to celebrate St John? Is it altogether necessary? Should we not leave it, because it is so strange, so foreign, so incomprehensible? What can we do? These questions are justified, I think, because a festival like St John – if its character is not to revert to pre-Christian times – needs renewal. But there is no doubt that it is a very important and necessary festival for the human soul, because otherwise Rudolf Steiner would not have given us the St John's Imagination – an immense image accompanied with the words that resound from the heights, the depths and from our very own inner being.[1] Rudolf Steiner would not have spoken at such length and so often about the being of John the Baptist; he even concluded his last lecture with a vast image of the path that this being has taken throughout the ages until about one hundred years ago.[2]

So there is no need to ask whether we should celebrate St John's. The only question is how? And it is not a single, simple answer that can be given to this 'how'. Because a festival is a being, a great being, and one that has many different facets: indeed, every year it has a new countenance, and it is on us to learn to behold it and to understand it. It is not often that in spite of the fact that nature around us does not give herself in the true joy-like mood and fashion that St John can be experienced so strongly, so imminently, so directly as this year. During the past days I have sometimes had the impression that it is good that clouds come and go, because otherwise we would hardly be able to stand the overwhelming strength and power of the light. The light that draws human souls out of their paths, which makes us spread into the far widths of existence and give ourselves up entirely because the strength to hold oneself within is diminished – especially during this very sunny year.[3]

Therefore, I have the impression that it would be good if we turn to one special aspect of St John's time, in order to create a balance to this overpowering force of expansion. A balance through turning inward, in looking back and in reminding ourselves of what has happened during the last nine months as spiritual deed, as common work and study within this hall. Because it is the first time that we can be together at St John's here in our hall. And it is just nine months since we had opened it – two hundred and eighty days. If we look back and try to remember the different steps we took throughout these past nine months, it might help us to understand where we are and where we have come from. So let us remember together, the spiritual path that we have walked together throughout these past nine months. I will not speak about all the important everyday activities in our hall – the lessons with the children, the Sunday services, the plays for the children, the celebrations of the festivals, the plays on our stage, all this is not unimportant. But today we will look back to our common spiritual work. We look back first of all to the first lecture that took place here in this room. It was on September 23 that the first lecture could be given in this hall on the theme of 'historic conscience' – a theme that already foreshadowed the moment at which we have now arrived. Some of you might remember how we tried earnestly to come to a certain insight of what Rudolf Steiner calls the 'historic conscience' in the lecture on the St John Imagination. We turned to the course of history and we saw, standing behind historic events, the leading archangels, seven in number, who were the time-spirits for certain epochs: Gabriel, Samael, Raphael, Zacharael, Anael, Oriphiel and Michael. And we came to understand that Uriel, the archangelic spirit who rules over the height of summer in which historic conscience should come into consciousness in every human being, is not one of the seven. Instead, he weaves the deeds of the other seven archangels as historic conscience into the historic epochs of *all* human existence. With this we ended, calling upon the whole historic development of humanity – feeling ourselves one with it, and being aware of the fact that Michael himself is the time-spirit of our current epoch.

Then, in preparation for Advent and for Christmas, we occupied ourselves with the word within the human being. We tried to understand the human being as bearer of the word as a speaking being, and how this is exceptionally special and significant for human beings on earth. All this work was crowned when, during the Holy Nights, we turned to the Cosmic Word itself, trying to draw nearer to a first understanding of the working of the Cosmic Word in human beings as well as in nature. And I may remind you how we likened minerals and stones to gestures, how we likened plants to mimicry, and how we compared the animals to the physiognomy of nature, thereby seeing more and more the Cosmic Word at work within nature: the Logos appearing as gesture in stones, as mimic in the plants, as physiognomy in the animals. And then this Rosicrucian meditation 'The Stones Are Mute'[4] became a guide for all our deliberations. In the end these meditative words – about stones and plants, animals and human beings, soul and spirit, and all this just being the Cosmic Word – led us to a comprehension of the first Goetheanum, which Rudolf Steiner himself called the House of the Word. We were able to liken each of the verses of this meditation to the secret figures and forms of the windows of the Goetheanum. We moved from the west towards the east, as it were, until the last verse gave us the possibility to comprehend the statue of the Representative of Mankind: to look at this and behold in it the Logos incarnate. But at the same time we discovered that the Representative of Mankind, walking forwards, creates his spirit-space by warding off the powers of evil.

This gave us the indication for our further work in preparing the weeks of Lent leading towards Easter. For the first time we dared to occupy ourselves with the problem of evil. And we studied as intensively as possible the different sides of evil. We learned to see and understand the power of egoism. We spoke of the seven deadly sins. We tried to understand the drives of the sins in connection with the powers of the elements – with life and sound, with light and warmth, with air and water and earth. This led our gaze beneath the surface of the earth, and we began to comprehend the inner spheres that keep the earth together through the powers of evil and the resistance inherent in it. And with this image we went towards Easter, and we tried to understand what it means that on the day after Good Friday the Christ descended into the Earth, permeating the nine evil spheres, in order to rise as the Risen One on Easter Sunday. From then on, throughout the forty days, he accompanied his disciples and apostles. We tried to follow this in looking again to the statue of the Representative of Mankind and learning to understand the Easter Imagination. There Raphael speaks to the human being, explaining the work of the spirit within the forces of nature.

Then came the ten days between Ascension and Whitsun. During this period we tried to discover the five sources of spiritual science: where they come from, and how they unite to create what Rudolf Steiner gave to the world as a revelation of the being of Anthroposophia. We found these five sources expressed in the work of special personalities – Eduard Schuré, Friedrich Nietzsche, Karl Julius Schröer, Ernst Haeckel and Rudolf Steiner himself – and we named them Theosophy, Anthroposophy, Goetheanism, the new Christ impulse, and the new teaching of reincarnation and karma. And again, behind these five lectures there rose up for us the image of the Goetheanum. There were the two huge cupolas with the painted images of the past and the present and the future of human evolution; there were the pillars, the architraves, the windows; there was the figure of the Representative of Mankind. And we could almost see and imagine how these five sources, these five streams of inspiration, found their image and expression within this building which, for a few years, stood on the hill of Dornach.

We concluded this series of lectures with a sixth about the story of the 'Rock Spring Wonder',[5] imagining the cup as the actual secret, the true mystery of human beings on Earth, standing here, filled with karma, but given reincarnation as their task. And then came Whitsun, and we were graced to be able to behold and to imbue ourselves with eurythmy; with the word appearing here on the stage in a most wonderful form.

If we now look back and try to understand where and how the spirit has led us, is it possible to say something that might help us see all these different steps in a common light? I think it is possible, because whatever we did, whatever we attempted to do, whatever we were striving for, I can only see it as though we were trying to regain the lost word. We tried to find again some approach towards the Cosmic Word. And as soon as we realise this, we can refer back to my last lecture when I pointed out how during the time of Ancient Egypt (around 2000–1500 BC) initiates were no longer able to reach through their initiation the sphere of Cosmic Sound and Cosmic Word, and how they returned and called themselves 'The Sons of the Widow', because Isis had become a widow.[6] She could no longer show to her sons – to her pupils – the way to Osiris, her brother and husband. And still it is so that the Word, the Cosmic Word is lost. Whichever step we take in spiritual science, whichever way we try to go, whatever goal we want to reach, it means to regain the Word, the Cosmic Word, the Logos, which is still lost.

Now St John's time has come, and again the question stands before us as I have pointed out: 'What is St John's?' And with that I mean St John's as a festival. You see, from the first Advent Sunday onwards until the time of Whitsun, we are graced by the power of the Christian festivals. If we want, our soul can be imbued with the grace and wonder of these Christian festivals that follow each other. The preparation during Advent for the birth of the light, the birth of the Logos, at Christmas; then, after Christmas, accompanying the Logos through its deeds here on earth, through the darkness of the earth, on the way towards Golgotha and death on the cross; then the descent into the Earth, the resurrection, and the glory and wonder of the forty days between Ascension and Whitsun, culminating in the outpouring of the Holy Spirit over the disciples of the Lord. This is the Christian year, the true spiritual year that takes place anew every year.

But after Whitsun this comes to an end, and to try to build the bridge from Whitsun to St John is a rather futile attempt. It cannot work, even if there are only a few days remaining between Whitsun and St John's. Last year we had a few weeks, but however late Whitsun is, due to a late

Easter, there is a break, a complete hiatus, because with St John's something entirely new begins. We must learn more and more to understand what this means.

Let us ask what happens now at St John's time. It is the summer solstice; the sun begins to sink lower and the days become shorter, and although the height of summer is still to come, nevertheless the sun begins to withdraw from the Earth, and the Earth withdraws from the sun. This is what happens after the glory and wonder of Whitsun. And yes, it has to happen. It has to happen because every time a human being comes to birth they have to undergo nine months of development within their mother's womb before they are born. We cannot forego this of course. Every time we come down to Earth, for every new incarnation, we have to undergo this process. We have to dive into the depths, filled with the powers of the cosmos, to build up our own body again. But with specific purpose the body is then born, and then, after the steps of birth and further development, we can walk on for a few decades again in fulfilling our task here on Earth. This has to happen, and not just for human beings, but it also for each year.

Let us try to understand that the year is a being. 1960 is a being and 1961 is a being. Since the birth of Christ, 1,963 yearly earthly beings have been born into the evolving stream of humanity. This is the cycle of the year; the year is born between Whitsun and St John's. This year – 1960 – becomes, from Christmas onwards, the year 1961 [spoken whilst drawing on the blackboard]. The year 1961 grows into the year 1962, which in turn is also born. And again 1962 goes on and now we are at the time when the year 1963 – as a spiritual aptitude, as the destiny of millions of karmic events – is born into the world and is preparing the future of humanity.

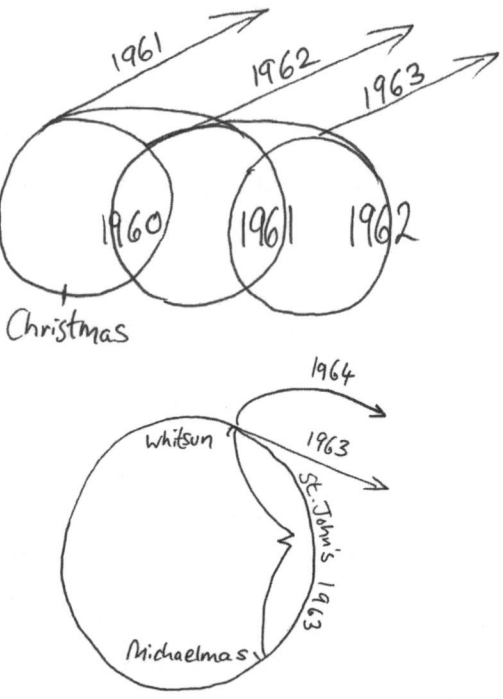

Sketches based on blackboard drawings done at the time.

You will understand what I mean if I try to be more explicit. Let us say that this is the year 1963 [the second drawing], which is born just in this time between Whitsun and St John's. One part of 1963 – let me call it the 'natural' part of 1963 – is now turning downwards. The spiritual part of 1963 has turned upwards. It is born. From now on the year 1963 is freed up, it is going upwards, it has its destiny. But the earthly year now, during the time of the three months from St John's until Michaelmas, prepares the reception of the seed of the coming year, 1964. From Michaelmas 1963, within the womb, the year 1964 will be born, will develop, unfold and be born after Whitsun 1964. One year within the other, one year beside the other, with all its beinghood, with all its destiny, with all its weakness or power. This is the mystery and the riddle of this time between Whitsun and St John's. St John's day takes the natural year and plants it down into the course of the earth, into the course of the seasons: thus the spiritual year is born with human beings and their destiny, with all its events. And now we can read the words of the Uriel Imagination in a new way, and imagine a third element appearing between the Spirit-Father above and the Mother in the 'matter' of the Earth below with the words:

> Behold our weaving,
> the kindling radiance,
> the warming life.

It is filled with light and warmth in expansion. And down below:

> Live in the earth's sustaining,
> and in the form-giving breathing,
> with the power of true being.

And in between is the human being with their own soul:

> Feel the limbs of Man,
> from the heavens illuminated,
> in the strength of worlds united.

What can this mean? Within the cloak, the garment of this trinity in nature, this trinity within the substance of light and warmth, of stone and water – within this bounty of all nature, filled with the powers of the Father, held by the threads of the Mother – within this the new seed for the coming year, the new being of 1964, is implanted into the womb of the Earth, and there it rests. It waits until July, August and September have gone, until humans have harvested the fruits they have planted, until the plants have given thanks through their fruits to the powers of health. As soon as in the coming autumn the Earth begins to contemplate its own being, the spirit that has been implanted into this trinity of existence, the spirit that has spread around us, begins to unfold. The embryo of the new year begins to develop step by step. At Christmas it begins to spread its wings, at Easter it already tries to be born, but only at Whitsun is the shell broken open, and all our destiny, all our deeds, all our faults, all our sins, are born with this year. And here these words sound:

> Substances are densified,
> errors are rectified,
> hearts are sifted.

Here it appears, becomes apparent, because into it our deeds, our words, our reasoning are all inscribed. From now on they go out into the world, unredeemed, until we ourselves, when being born again, meet them and can redeem what we have done wrong or gather as fruits that which we have done right. Personal karma is born within the spiritual body of the year, it comes to birth during these days between Whitsun and St John's. St John points in this direction, saying: 'Start again! Begin anew, become humble, natural; try again and never give in!' Every year in August the beheading of St John is repeated, because the earth draws away from the sun, and the sun draws away from the earth. St John has to start anew. Every year his spirit is born and rises to become the group soul of the disciples; he enters into Lazarus and becomes the other John. In this way we can begin to understand how St John in his twofold way prepares withing himself all that happens to his other being, to Lazarus–John. And now you can read again the introductory words of the gospel, which this John has written, and read it with this background:

> In the beginning was the Word, and the Word was with God, and the Word was God. The same was in the beginning with God. All things were made by him, and without him was not anything made that was made. In him was life, and the life was the light of man. In him was life, and the life was the light of men. And the light shineth in the darkness, and the darkness comprehended it not. There was a man, sent from God, whose name was John.

But John the Baptist, though he starts again and will be beheaded again, is every time succeeded by the writer of the gospel who knows 'In the beginning was the Word', but who also knows that 'there was a man, whose name was John', knowing that it was he himself.

In this the mysteries of this time of the year are embedded, as the time now comes when our soul will, so to speak, be given up to the light and be transformed within nature, and only towards Michaelmas, when the new seed for the coming year also begins to unfold, only then can our search for the lost word start again. I have the impression that it should more and more become a custom to look back to the last nine months after we have reached the summit of the year on St John's Day. We can look back in order to learn what we need to understand: the shape and form of this destiny, the destiny of the being that is this year, which has just been born at this time. And we look forward to the coming year – now to the year 1964 – which spiritually is already formed out within the vast image of the trinity around us, finding its place within the womb of Mother Earth.

With this we can conclude with words by Rudolf Steiner, which might help us in our search for the lost word:

> The stars spake once to human beings;
> It is World destiny
> That they are silent now.
> To be aware of the silence
> Can become pain for earthly humans.
>
> But in the deepening silence
> There grows and ripens
> What humankind speaks to the stars.
> To be aware of this speaking
> Can become strength for Spirit-Man.[7]

Let us hope, dear friends, that more and more we will be able to engender words that will speak again to the stars, and that we will strengthen our way to perceive what we speak, and thereby help to create a new world.

Individual and Historic Conscience

Lecture in Spring Valley, July 21, 1962

Dear friends

This is a kind of memorial lecture, a tribute to our friend Ehrenfried Pfeiffer who, for many years, held the summer school opening lecture, and whose great concern all his life was for the earth.[1]

It was one of the very great tasks of Rudolf Steiner to enlighten humanity on the existence of historic conscience, alongside the individual kind, and he explained the development of conscience especially in connection with memory. From the beginning of anthroposophy until almost the very end of his life, Rudolf Steiner time and again brought up this great problem, presenting it in the light of different aspects and from different points of view. One of his last letters was on memory and conscience.[2] He was the first one to point out that conscience was not a gift bestowed on humanity from the beginning, but from a certain time onwards the voice of conscience more and more developed deep within the human being. Now the time has come when a new form of conscience is developing in connection with the Spirit of the Earth.

In October 1923, Rudolf Steiner gave a description of historic conscience, which appears in the great imagination of midsummer when the archangels Gabriel, Uriel and Michael are weaving and working in Nature.[3]

Let it be our task tonight to find out about the individual and historic conscience of the whole human race. How and in which way did the sudden appearance of conscience in history happen? Out of his special connection to historical knowledge Rudolf Steiner spoke of it from a very specific side in 1909[4] and makes a comment about the fact that there was not even a word for conscience in ancient cultures. Just one moon node later, in 1928, the rector of the University of Jena, Professor Zucker, gave a lecture on *syneidesis-conscientia*, speaking of the development of the Greek term, and later the word 'conscience', similar to the way in which Rudolf Steiner had referred to it.[5]

In 1909 Rudolf Steiner had pointed to the dramas of Aeschylus about Orestes, who is persecuted by the Erinyes after murdering his mother. He is still clairvoyant and sees them coming after him, torturing him. This was in 508 BC. One hundred years later, Euripides, in his drama, does not show Orestes being persecuted, but instead having a conversation with Menelaos, who asks: What is this illness like that troubles you? What kind of sickness leads you to such destruction? Orestes answers: My conscience, for being conscious of having done some evil. *Syneidesis* in Greek means that I become conscious that I have done something evil. But from this time on an entirely new experience in the human soul began. The Erinyes were no longer seen as beings external to one's own soul, instead an inner voice began to sound. Through the experience of this voice Orestes says that he has become conscious. In this connection the initial common stem of the two-fold form of conscience is thus mentioned. These two interconnected experiences are of great importance, and so we have the two words: conscience and consciousness.

The first one who heard this voice, one hundred years

before the Greek drama, was Elijah in the Old Testament. It is clear that he no longer hears the word of Yahweh from outside, neither in the clouds, nor in the wind; but in the silent harbour of his own existence, there the word of God began to speak. Four hundred years later the inner voice of conscience was to become more and more the organ for the recognition of Christ. Indeed, in the coming two thousand years this development will continue. In the meantime there is a tremendous amount of literature about the development of conscience. One could spend hours quoting what various philosophers have said about human conscience, but the more we research our time, the more we realise that conscience does not continue to be the quiet, admonishing voice within us, but instead has become something different – it really is developing further. Karl Jaspers says (and I quote in my own words from the German) that with my conscience I experience a distance to myself. I am not confined to my own existence but can take steps to penetrate to the hidden background of my existence. Conscience is one of these steps.[6]

Now we begin to understand what Rudolf Steiner describes in his St John's Imagination about the being of the archangel Uriel. He, being filled with all that keeps the universe together, turns his earnest gaze towards the shadowing clouds within the cosmic Will. There he beholds the mistakes, the sins and the lies of human beings. We can try to imagine the cosmic Intelligence above us and the cosmic Will below us, filled with our misdeeds, and between them, in the centre of the image so to speak, the countenance of Uriel. This image of the time of year we are now in can permeate us through our strength of imagination and Uriel and his countenance can appear to us.

In the Greek tragedy of Euripides the word conscience appeared for the first time. Through preparation in the mysteries the voice of conscience was gradually developed and slowly became known by thousands of people, who first had to experience within their own soul the tension between fear and compassion.

In the same way we can have the experience each summer that our souls can go up to the heights, and, as we are also told by the *Calendar of the Soul*, we can lose ourselves; but then we look down into the depths described in the Imagination and see our mistakes, our misdeeds. It is a similar experience as that of fear on the one hand and compassion on the other. Two thousand years ago, conscience appeared as the centre between the heights and the depths of our existence, between fear and compassion. The light of conscience, this awareness, belongs to the possibility not only to be one's own individuality, but also to be conscious of being a self.

In the Imaginations for the seasons, Rudolf Steiner taught us about the silver from below and the gold from above, and how they work together to form in August and September the shining armour of the archangel Michael, mirrored through nature to human experience. If we take it earnestly, we are able to say: historic conscience is the power of Michael himself, who appears in his armour; silver from below, gold from above. Michael takes on the faults and transforms them into the gold of intelligence. Michael himself, step by step, brought the cosmic intelligence down to earth, which had formerly resided only in the realm of the gods. He brought it streaming down to human beings, but must guard it until human beings are able to add their will, their conscience, to this consciousness. It is our task to learn to understand it, to become conscious of the development of the human being and therefore take responsibility for it. Michael can only present us with this possibility and leave us to freely choose it if we will, when, year after year, as summer turns into autumn, he revives the power of the historic conscience. Otherwise the consciousness for world development, and particularly the will to take true responsibility, remains weak in our time.

At midsummer we can experience the gaze of Uriel as cosmic intelligence appears in full glory. But at the same time historic conscience appears, judging the faults of human beings, and with silver from the depths and gold from the heights, Michael's armour is formed. Into our hearts and minds, cosmic intelligence and historic conscience flow together. They are sent by the archangels of the time leading from midsummer into autumn. Michael and Uriel give each other their hands; they work together in order to save evolution from the same misdeeds that once had been committed in Atlantean times, when mystery knowledge was misused. And we can be sure that cosmic intelligence is being misused in our time because human beings are not yet able to turn properly to experience the archangels as they express themselves throughout the seasons each year. Michael, in the service of the one who went through the Mystery of Golgotha, takes on these sins of humanity, sins continually committed by us.

We can now let the words of the Imagination sound with this background:

> Substances are densified
> Errors are judged and rectified
> Hearts are sifted.
>
> Substances are condensed from below
> Faults are judged from above
> in the light of the cosmic intelligence
> Hearts are sifted and absolved by historic conscience,
> whose bearer and carrier is Michael.

To conclude, however, we still need to answer one

question: why does Rudolf Steiner not refer to the person of John in the midsummer Imagination? Because it is no longer the Festival of John! It has taken on an entirely new meaning! The Imagination speaks of the Trinity – above and below and the meeting of the two – but it does not any more call on John the Baptist who has become the Evangelist.

Whose festival is it then? It is really the festival of the one who became Christianised through the initiation of human conscience: it is Paul's! The one from whom we hear he was 'born out of due time' (1 Cor 15:8). But it is more than just this. It is the one who gave birth to the new power of conscience, and with this he was far ahead of his time. And so we can say with Paul – it is not only 'I' and consciousness of the 'I', but something else that can be born within us. 'Not I, but the Cosmic Word in me.'

As we have already said, conscience brings about a kind of distance to ourselves: I and myself are no longer identical, they do not fall together. On the one hand we are in doubt about ourselves through ego consciousness, but on the other we not only know we are an 'I am', an individual, but in that knowing we also know that being an individual is something more than just being ourselves.

Thomas Aquinas, in his *Summa*, says that we know with the help of Reason, but we acknowledge that which we know with the help of conscience. We can almost say in an image: conscience is like a lantern, a light that shines in us and upon us and gives us the consciousness of ourselves. We and our conscience are both present in our consciousness, and that has widened out our ego experience. It is conscience that has allowed us to develop as human beings, to become human.

Yet Rudolf Steiner speaks of historic conscience, not just personal, individual conscience. He reminds us that it is not possible to look upon the earnest countenance of Uriel, gazing towards the depths of Earth, without also seeing there something that might be described as wing-like arms or arm-like wings, in an attitude of earnest admonition.[7] This seems to be the gesture that brings down into the human race what we can call historic conscience, something that we know too little of in our present age because it relates to the whole of humanity in the same way that individual conscience relates to the individual. The development of human beings is linked to world development. Referring to the midsummer imagination, Rudolf Steiner describes how with clairvoyant possibilities, gazing into the centre of the Earth, one can see how everything is filled with a kind of blue power, a strength in which we can discern silver-like threads that appear with forms like crystals, geometrical silver forms of crystals. What is this 'bluish strength'? It is nothing but cosmic will. We tread on cosmic will on this earth, we are permeated by cosmic will. But if we behold the light that radiates in to the summer clouds, we see something like cosmic gold threads, rays of gold. And if we ask ourselves what it is this gold, there is only one answer – it is cosmic intelligence.

Cosmic intelligence	these two weave together, silver and gold; they unite and then turn again to earth.
Cosmic will	

[It seems that Karl König must have drawn something on the blackboard at this stage, but it has not been included in the notes.]

Rudolf Steiner then describes a countenance appearing within the light clouds, a countenance with earnest eyes, looking down on the bluish strength. This countenance is Uriel, who gazes down into the ground of earth and within the cosmic will sees something new. He sees dark clouds, the polar opposite of the light summer clouds; they are the faults, the mistakes, the the sins of human beings.

Now we may ask, who is Uriel? And it is really a question of if we are permitted to ask, because for centuries occultists did not even mention him. Helena Blavatsky only refers to him once or twice, though she often speaks of the other archangels. It seems that Uriel has receded into the background of human consciousness. In the Book of Enoch, however, Uriel is the main figure, and we now know that the Essenes at Qumran had as their main study material the Book of Enoch. If we were able to ask one of them who Uriel was, he would quote many sayings from Enoch. Uriel was the archangel whom God sent to Noah to prepare for the great Flood, the messenger who brought tidings that the decision had been taken to bring about the destruction of Atlantis because people had diverted and misused mystery knowledge. Uriel was the messenger of historic conscience who told Noah know to build the Ark and thus save a certain number of human beings with Mystery wisdom. This same person could also tell us that it was Uriel who showed Enoch the place where the Luciferic angels were imprisoned and held for a time to safeguard the continued progress of humanity. He could tell us that Uriel was also the one who was the keeper of all the laws of the stars; in fact, the whole cosmos is in the keeping of Uriel. And if we could hear this from one of the Qumran Essenes, we would understand better the description that Rudolf Steiner uses in the midsummer Imagination: Uriel, whose own intelligence is in reality composed of the forces of the planets and the fixed stars of the zodiac, who preserves cosmic thought in his own thought.

Uriel is cosmic intelligence. He is the weaving together of the planets and the stars, he is the bearer and guardian of the forces streaming to earth from out of the Word: the consonants of the fixed stars and the vowels of the planets, they all sound together in Uriel's mind and become actual being. They may also become being within our own souls, where they can be discovered more and more by thought and become conscious. When that happens we take on responsibility for the Word living within us; we have developed historic conscience.

A Michaelmas Lecture, 1965

Föhrenbühl, September 28, 1965

My dear friends

The festival of St Michael is extraordinarily diverse, as are the other great festivals of the year. And one can have the impression that it wears a different garment each year because it is so diverse and can reveal itself in all manner of guises and forms, and yet remains with its inner content nevertheless Michaelic.

A year ago for instance we came together to discuss specific content for the festival, and I think that we also managed to find something of significance in the deep connection between architecture and the social activity of community building.[1] We began to find understanding for what it meant to be a freemason in the Middle Ages. That meant that someone was not only initiated into the secrets of architecture, which enabled them to build churches and houses, but at the same time was committed to the innermost questions of social structures for humanity. During last year's work – it was on September 28, exactly one year ago – we turned to the fact that it was just at that moment, that point in world history when the first Goetheanum went up in flames, that Rudolf Steiner gave us indications about the working of Michael and the powers of community building that stream out of his being. He started to talk about the necessity of renewing the Michaelmas festival for the sake of the future development of the human being. It was on May 23, 1923, in Berlin that he said the following:

> More important than all other reflections on social conditions – which can only lead to results in our present chaotic conditions if they include the spirit – would be this: that a number of people with understanding for these things should come together to institute on Earth, in accord with the cosmos, a *Michael festival*. This autumn festival would be a worthy counterpart to the Easter festival. If people could take the initiative and found a festival whose source arises only in the spiritual world, but which can kindle feelings of fellowship among human beings – a festival whose immediacy and reality would be created through the fresh, full power of the human heart – then something would come into being which can unite people once more in the social realm. In the past, festivals used to bind human beings strongly together. Just think, for instance, of all that has been done and said and thought in connection with festivals for the whole of civilisation; all of it entered physical life through festivals established directly out of the spirit.
>
> If people could take the initiative to establish a Michael festival worthy of the name, during the last days of September, this would be a most significant deed. But they would have to find the courage within themselves not merely to discuss such things as external social reforms, but to do something that connects the earth with the heavens, that re-connects physical with spiritual conditions. If the spirit was led down once more in to earthly conditions, this would give humanity a mighty impetus for the continuation of all life and civilisation.[2]

Now this was a challenge that Rudolf Steiner's pupils, meaning us, have hardly been able to fulfil at all really. And this task still awaits our activity to create such festivals, Michaelic festivals, that would connect people to each other in the right way. Those of you who were able to experience the festivities at the Lehenhof over the past few days will perhaps have felt moved by the various events that took place there and which could give a glimpse of what could be meant by a future Michaelmas festival in social life.[3]

Through Rudolf Steiner we can experience the Parable of the Great Banquet as the gospel connected to Michaelmas. In this parable, which comes in the middle of the Gospel of Luke, Christ tells his disciples how a wealthy man arranges a wedding for his son. He invites his friends and sends his servants out to ask them to come to the feast. But his friends are all indisposed. Three times the man sends his servants out, but three times we are told the invited guests cannot attend because they believe they have more important things to attend to: work, family, financial matters and so on, just the sort of things that people believe they need in order to fulfil their lives here on earth. And so the man sends his messengers out and tells them to go to the streets and invite everyone they find there: rich and poor, beggars and those who cannot walk, whoever they could find. A little bit of this atmosphere one could feel these days when one moved about amongst the hundreds of the most diverse, special, or also not so special, people. But it was like a starting point.

But now I would like to try and approach this Michaelmas festival from a completely different angle than last year. I want, however, to keep the social question in the centre because the main question of our times – the central challenge to our whole being – is the struggle for social renewal. And if that does not begin to be found in

A MICHAELMAS LECTURE, 1965

the course of our times then the necessary renewal of the human being will not be possible. And here I do refer to 'times' and not simply to 'time', because it will be a long process. But this is the task of our times, meaning the time period of Michael. And this needs to come to our awareness right now as we stand at the entrance to the Michaelmas festival.

During the summer two outstanding personalities of present creative and cultural life have entered the portal of death: one at the beginning and one at the end of summer. On June 13 the Jewish philosopher and writer Martin Buber died at a ripe age of eighty-seven in Jerusalem, and, at the beginning of this month, during the night from September 4 to 5, the Christian physician Albert Schweitzer crossed the threshold in Lambarene, at the high age of ninety. I am sure all of you will at least know the names of these two personalities; I know that many of you know more about Martin Buber and Albert Schweitzer. The question presents itself, in which way could these two significant personalities be connected to each other, and what could their deaths have to do with the Michaelmas festival of 1965?

Let us cautiously and step-by-step approach what I have in mind for this year, it is something that is close to my heart. Martin Buber was born in Vienna in 1878. He came from an extraordinarily complex and difficult family background, and this led to him being sent from Vienna to live with his grandparents in what was then called Lemberg. Lemberg was at the time the capital city of the Austrian province of Galicia, which was really eastern Europe, and today it is partly in Poland and partly in Russia.* At that time it was a province of the Austro-Hungarian Empire, a huge proportion of the inhabitants were Polish Jews, Polish and

---

* Today it is Lviv in west Ukraine.

Ukrainian farmers, and Austrian troops. Martin Buber's grandfather was a rich but also highly educated man, deeply occupied with the Jewish esoteric doctrine, the Kabbalah, and with the Jewish Midrash. This was the milieu, the atmosphere, in which Martin Buber grew up. It seems that he was deeply influenced in quite a natural way by the outstanding personality of his grandfather. He studied at various universities and was rich enough to not have to worry about finding a profession. In 1925, already at a mature age, he started as professor for History of the Jewish Religion and Jewish Ethics at the university in Frankfurt am Main, where he stayed until the barbaric times began in central Europe and went then as Professor of Sociology and Social History to the University of Jerusalem. From there he travelled extensively and was on familiar terms with just about all the leading people of modern culture.

If one looks back on all that Martin Buber has published then one sees something of his main concern, what was most important to him; one can see in a twofold direction. On the one hand he was concerned with a renewal of the German language in connection with the Old Testament. Within a period of fourteen years he did a completely new translation of the whole of the Old Testament, and did this in a really unusual way, working together with the prominent linguist Franz Rosenzweig. The result was sixteen volumes of translation. And if one reads this, one can really experience a re-creation of the contents of the Old Testament in contrast to the Luther translation.

On the other hand Buber had a thoroughly social concern, as he struggled right until his death with the question: how does one human being meet the other? How can it be possible at all that I, in spite of being so enclosed within myself, manage to connect to the other person? One of his first and most important books, first published in 1923, was *Ich und Du* (later published in

English as *I and Thou*), which laid the foundation for the whole of his social philosophy and his struggle with the question of human encounter. Today I was very touched as Dr von Arnim mentioned this fundamental social question in his introductory words because this has so much to do with Martin Buber's inner struggle with the connection between I and You.[4] It is indeed one of the most important questions of our time in connection to behaviour (and misbehaviour) of the human being. The task is the re-building of interpersonal relationships.

Albert Schweitzer was of a different stature. He was a personality that brought a great deal with him. By the time he was thirty he had already lived something quite like a whole life; indeed, it was even something more like two lives, because around 1905 he gave up everything he had done up to then in order to study medicine. Yet he was already well known in both areas of his life. He was a musician and had done a tremendous amount for the renewal of interpretation of Bach's music, he had renewed the craft of organ making and written a comprehensive history on it, and he had presented one of the most prominent biographies of Bach – in two volumes. At the same time, almost as though incidentally, he had been Professor of Protestant Theology at the university of Strasbourg where he had written a significant work on the history of research into the life of Jesus. He was one of the first in modern times to point to the importance of turning once more to eschatological studies in order to understand the life of Jesus. He argued that we can only begin to understand the events in Palestine of two thousand years ago if we grasp the fact that a quest to experience the spirit of God continued throughout the whole of Judaism, indeed throughout he whole of human history. An enormously strong chiliasm filled the soul life of people in those times, and Christ – this is how Albert Schweitzer presented it –

came to fulfil this chiliastic seething in the human soul. Christ had expected the coming of the Kingdom of God and the Last Judgement, but because this did not happen the church was founded to take its place. Now this was an extraordinary point of view, and through this Albert Schweitzer advanced into the front rows of protestant theology, which was quite significant at that time. That was his life up to his thirtieth year.

Then Schweitzer heard about the suffering of the indigenous peoples in Africa and cast aside everything he had achieved to return to the school desk and study medicine. He became a physician and went to Lambaréné in western Gabon in 1913. That was his second life so to speak. He was there until his recent death.

We should not forget to mention that both personalities, Martin Buber as well as Albert Schweitzer, have been defamed in the most malicious fashion by a modern generation that knows everything better and yet does not know better than this sort of incomprehensible and mean attack. Schweitzer was defamed because of his medical work,[5] Martin Buber because of his cosmopolitanism.[6]

But we can ask the question: where did these two find the source for their thought and working? How could it happen that Schweitzer pushed everything aside that he had achieved to take this solitary step to become a missionary physician in Africa and begin a hospital in the middle of the jungle? And where did Buber's insights come from? If we follow these questions we come to something special and perhaps significant, although very unusual. Buber, before he had started with the themes I mentioned – translating the Bible and researching human interrelations – had tried to re-awaken a certain spiritual stream, or at least to awaken awareness of it and to show its relevance for the development of German culture. Indeed he was the first and, for a long time, the only one to refer to the important stream of Jewish Hasidism. I am sure that Rudolf Steiner would have attached great importance to it if one of his pupils had looked into this more thoroughly. He actually did give this task specifically to one of the priests of the Christian Community, because, as Rudolf Steiner himself said, it originates from something of great significance.[7]

What is Hasidism? I cannot go into all the details now, but let me just say briefly that at the beginning and middle of the eighteenth century, Hasidism attempted to resolve the rigidity that had set into Jewish religious life and Jewish regulations. It was a sort of mystical movement that was inaugurated by a rabbi using the name Baal Shem Tov, although his real name was actually Rabbi Israel Ben Eliezer.[8] The pupils of Baal Shem Tov tasked themselves with inner exercises, mystic immersion in order to find direct connection to the Godhead once more. Whoever thus became a 'Zaddik', a 'righteous one', or initiate, would have the task of kindling three things in their pupils: humility, joy and something that was called ecstasy, or one could say 'entrancement'. Do not think that there were just a few hundred of these Hasidim. For about one hundred years this movement for renewal, this chiliastic movement, affected thousands and thousands of Jewish communities, tens of thousands of Jewish people in Galicia, in Poland, Belarus. I myself remember stories my father told me, as he was the son of one of the last Hasidim,[9] and remember how one could still discern something of the mystical power that must have once lived in that movement.[10]

Rabbi Israel Ben Eliezer, the great Baal Shem Tov, lived from around 1699 to 1760. The dates are not so exactly known, and anyone who knows about protestant history will have already noticed that it coincides almost exactly with the life of Count Zinzendorf. The founder and creator of the Herrnhuter Brotherhood lived from 1700 until 1760. This brotherhood was a real child of pietism, but just imagine how it must have been at that time. At the beginning of the eighteenth century, not only in Central but also in Eastern Europe, and not only amongst Christians but also for Jewish people, a great movement of awakening arose.

Further to the east, far into Russia, something appeared around the same time that is known today as *staretsdom*, which was an attempt at renewal in the Orthodox Christian church. In both cases we see a turning inwards towards pietism, in Hasidism and in *staretsdom*. Out of these sources flowed the streams that were decisive for Martin Buber and Albert Schweitzer. If you follow up on their impulses you will find Martin Buber's roots in Hasidism, just as well as Albert Schweitzer's roots in that which arose from the pietism of the Herrnhuter Brotherhood – this was the background to the great missionary work that the latter personality created.

In the well-known publication *On the Edge of the Primeval Forests* by Albert Schweitzer, you can find, near to the beginning, how he describes the origins of his becoming a physician and moving to Lambaréné:

> I gave up my position of professor at the University in Strasbourg, as well as my literary work and my organ-playing, in order to go as a doctor to equatorial Africa. How did that come about?
>
> I had read about the physical miseries of the natives in the 'virgin forests', I had heard about them from missionaries, and the more I thought about it the stranger it seemed to me that we Europeans trouble ourselves so little about the great humanitarian task that offers itself to us in far-off lands. The parable of the rich man and Lazarus seemed to me to have been spoken directly of us! We are the rich man, for, through the advances of

medical science, we now know a great deal about disease
and pain, and have innumerable means of fighting
them, yet we take as a matter of course the incalculable
advantages which this new wealth gives us! Out there in
the colonies, however, sits wretched Lazarus, the native
folk, who suffers from illness and pain just as much as
we do, nay, much more, and has absolutely no means of
fighting them. And just as the rich man sinned against
the poor man at his gate because for want of thought
he never put himself in his place and let his heart and
conscience tell him what he ought to do, so do we sin
against the poor man at our gate.[11]

Out of these words something speaks to us that was Schweitzer's path: it was missionary work awakened from the pietistic heart. That was his concern. And from this a question arises for us. You see that both Albert Schweitzer and Martin Buber drank from the stream that flowed from the source of the movement of awakening at the beginning of the eighteenth century. So the question that arises is this: what was it that occurred at that point in the history of humanity, across the whole of Europe and into the East, that prompted people to suddenly turn inwards?

I believe that this fact has to do with something that worked its way into the foreground of historic development, which otherwise always lives and works in the background. We can see that there are two levels of historic development – one that unfolds in the foreground and one that is more concealed.[12] Rudolf Steiner once spoke about this concealed flow and called it the 'stream of sacrifice'. In that lecture he said the following:

We find the external civilisation which we know today, untouched by forces of clairvoyance. It is a civilisation whose knowledge of nature and her laws is assumed to be as useful for finding a philosophical basis for the secrets of existence as it is for making armaments. But we no longer feel that this kind of mental culture requires a sacrifice – we no longer feel that in order to achieve this mental culture we must offer sacrifice in a deeper sense to the higher spiritual Beings who direct the supra-sensible worlds. These sacrifices are in fact being made, but we are as yet too inattentive to notice them. The ancient Greek did notice that this external culture, which they traced back to Agamemnon, Menelaus, Odysseus, involved sacrifice; it is the daughter of the human spirit who in a certain way has to be sacrificed ever anew. And they represented this perpetual sacrifice demanded by intellectual culture as the sacrifice of Iphigenia, daughter of Agamemnon.

Thus to the question raised by the sacrifice of Iphigenia there resounds a wonderful answer! If nothing but that external culture, which can be traced back, as the ancient Greek understood it, to Agamemnon, Menelaus, Odysseus, were given to humanity, then under its influence our hearts, the deepest forces of souls, would have withered away. It is only because humanity retained the feeling that it should make perpetual sacrifice and should single out, set apart from this general intellectual culture, rites which, not superficially, but in a more profound sense, may be called sacerdotal – it is only because of this that this intellectual civilisation has been saved from drying up completely.[13]

We may therefore call this concealed stream running through the history of humanity the stream of the sacrifice of Iphigenia, but we can also call it the stream of Abel's sacrifice. This stream is usually concealed but comes occasionally into the light. At the beginning of the eighteenth century it revealed itself as an 'open secret' in pietism, in Hasidism, in *staretsdom*, and in many, many special individual personalities who really acted as priests during that time to create a counterbalance to the extraordinarily strong forces of rationalism that emerged during the first part of that century. This stream was in a way concealed and yet experienced as the Iphigenic stream of sacrifice in the way that Rudolf Steiner describes it, and which was not at all confined to ancient Greece.

The question remains, however, how it could be that such 'quiet citizens' became so manifold just at that time? What was happening in external history that made this development out of the inner stream of history so necessary as a counterbalance? There is a clear answer to this – it was the Thirty Years' War, which had left Europe a bleeding wound.[14] A third of the population was killed, more than half of their habitations had been burned to the ground or left in ruins. European peoples had fought, harassed and lacerated each other for decades, without sense or aim, in a manner that can only be compared in modern times to the senseless and purposeless destruction of the two World Wars. But beginning in the earliest part of the seventeenth century, in the year 1604, we see something arising that we can call the first open efforts of Rosicrucianism to influence and guide events. That is when the book about the social forms of the Fraternitas Rosae Crucis, the Brotherhood of the Rose Cross, first appeared. Then came the book *The Chymical Wedding of Christian Rosencreutz*, and, although it is mainly misunderstood and misinterpreted by historians today, one does know that these books had an extraordinary influence on certain individuals of the time. The intention behind this was to prevent the Thirty Years' War from breaking out. In exactly the same way that the Count of St Germain endeavoured to prevent the worst happening in the events that followed the French Revolution, so did the Rosicrucians act prior to the Thirty Years' War.

Both attempts were unsuccessful; the Thirty Years' War happened just as the French Revolution did, but despite this, what had been intended from the beginning of the seventeenth century onwards was not lost. Because, you see, it arose again. It arose as just this stream of pietism, of Hasidism and *staretsdom*, which attempted even more strongly and much more widely, to create peace, to unite peoples, and to gather together groups of people that could heal and bring joy and humility into the social settings of their time. True Rosicrucianism knows that no outer social structures can form the social fabric needed, but that all depends on the smallest, painstaking steps from one human being to another, from one circle of people to the other, from one group to another, and that these steps need as much social love as can be engendered, in order to create the leaven for the future forms of social life.

In this way we can trace back the working on Albert Schweitzer and Martin Buber, pietism and Hasidism. And we can thus see how, behind these two figures, something stood that had shown itself for the first time outwardly as Rosicrucianism, revealing itself in its urge into world history at the beginning of the seventeenth century. That is a great line drawn through the ages, which we cannot follow so very directly, but which we can perceive as a golden thread, weaving through the centuries.

Albert Schweitzer was born in 1875 and Martin Buber in 1878; in 1879 the current Michael Age began. Both Schweitzer and Buber are, so to speak, companions of this new beginning for our times, which strives for a renewal of civilisation.[15] I may just mention another special individual who was also born around the same time in 1876 – Ita Wegman. Another important person, Helen Keller, was born in 1880; it is the beginning of a renewal of all civilization in which humanity moves towards internalisation, towards inner development.

A MICHAELMAS LECTURE, 1965

If you study the beginnings of modern painting – whether you take the cubists, the futurists or whatever they call themselves – the Klees, Mackes, Marcks and Jawlenskys were all born around 1880. You can see that they are basically disposed towards becoming Michaelites. On the one hand there is a move towards internalisation, towards inner development, and on the other a drive to become socially active. Those two impulses are still central for our times, for the simple reason that they could not be fulfilled those forty, fifty, sixty, seventy years ago. We might ask, what is the problem when such prominent personalities as Schweitzer and Buber, as great as they were, could not break through to what could have been their Michaelism? Perhaps you will permit me to say the following.

At the beginning of this talk I mentioned that the parable of the Kingly Wedding (the great banquet) is the parable of the Michaelmas time. But this parable alone is not sufficient, because just to gather up the poor and disadvantaged is all well and good, but it does not lead us any further than the hospital in Lambaréné. It leads no further than all the many thousands of social initiatives of our time, even though I do see them as positive steps. But it does not lead us further if one thing is still missing. And I want to express that one thing in the image of another parable, namely that of the feeding of the five thousand. This is indeed the parable for our times, but the meaning of it is not that we should all have enough to eat, but that we should be fed by *spiritual* nourishment. The two fishes, the five loaves, the twelve baskets in which everything that was left over is collected, these are not meaningless numbers, nor is the feeding itself an image bound to a specific time. It is much more than that.

The two fishes are an image for 'I and Thou', for the encounter of one human being with the other and for that with which Martin Buber struggled. The five loaves represent the pentagram of the spiritual human being, the individual finding themselves in the spirit. And the twelve baskets are an image for the All, seen through the unity of the twelve pictures of the zodiac. All of that together is the new wisdom of the human being, namely, the wisdom of reincarnation and karma. Without that there can be no renewal of Christianity; without that there can be no renewal of our social existence, and without that there will be no renewal of social initiatives if the feeding of the five thousand does not take place. This means that people accept the fact that they originate from the spiritual world, live their lives on earth and then return to the spiritual world. If this does not become everyday knowledge then there will be no social renewal, and Christian renewal cannot take place. This is where both Martin Buber and Albert Schweitzer came to a halt.

It is strange that I got a letter from Albert Schweitzer just one year ago after I had sent him my little book about the Thalidomide catastrophe.[16] We never met personally but knew each other nevertheless and wrote to each other often.[17] He replied to me, saying:

> My dear colleague,
>
> I would like to give you my thanks for sending me your booklet about the Thalidomide catastrophe. I have read it with great interest over and again. You give us much to ponder about that we have as yet not really paid heed to. And what you write about the importance of empathy and love for the powers of healing we will indeed need to try and grasp. As yet we only have a first dull inkling about this.

You see, this is someone who has truly worked out of love and real human sacrifice, yet he has to write that all this is just 'a dull inkling' for him. He is not able to reach what a true Michaelite needs, which is to see how human beings originate from the spiritual world and descend to earthly existence in the light of individual destiny, and then to see that life enacted followed by a return to the spiritual world in order to descend once more, again and again, to this earth.

Rudolf Steiner gave very significant lectures in January, February and March of 1912 about reincarnation and karma.[18] If only they had been heard by more people! If only Albert Schweitzer, Martin Buber and hundreds of other leading cultural figures had taken this in, we would now be in such a different situation. In those lectures Rudolf Steiner says the following, and I do not want to quote him exactly but just to summarise in my words: It would actually be necessary for reincarnation and karma to penetrate into European consciousness in the same way that Copernicanism has found its way into the mind of every child, of every human being. Rudolf Steiner then asks, why does it have to be so difficult, why do human hearts have to ward off this quite natural insight that has been prepared for us by Goethe and Lessing and many others? Because Copernicanism is the result of the age of superficiality, where only knowledge of earthly spatial concepts is of interest; to understand reincarnation and karma involves a level of inner activity. The awakening call of the revivalist movements has gone before us, has prepared the way, but has been veiled; they found their way through again, and were again pushed aside. But now, in the age of Michael, knowledge of reincarnation and karma, which is Rosicrucian wisdom, must become connected to the light of Michael. Then new communities can be formed.

Dear friends, this should stand before our eyes and our hearts more and more, because all this can only take place if a new understanding of the human being is founded on the ground of human destiny and the paths that humanity takes between the spiritual and the earthly worlds. But it can only take place when such an understanding of the human being connects with the will for social renewal – meaning with the will for the Kingly Wedding or the Chymical Wedding.

What Schweitzer attempted in Lambaréné, what Buber struggled with, that can only find its fulfilment where spirit knowledge connects to the Michaelic will. This is what is expressed in the verse that Rudolf Steiner gave in his last address on September 28, 1924:

> Springing from Powers of the Sun,
> Radiant Spirit-powers, blessing all Worlds!
> For Michael's garment of rays
> Ye are predestined by Thought Divine.
>
> He, the Christ-messenger, revealeth in you –
> Bearing humanity aloft – the sacred Will of Worlds.
> Ye, the radiant Beings of Aether-Worlds,
> Bear the Christ-Word to humanity.
>
> Thus shall the Heralds of Christ appear
> To the thirstily waiting souls,
> To whom your Word of Light shines forth
> In cosmic age of Spirit-Man.
>
> Ye, the disciples of Spirit-Knowledge,
> Take Michael's Wisdom beckoning,
> Take the Word of Love of the Will of Worlds
> Into your soul's aspiring, actively![19]

Those are pieces of the loaves and the fishes, of reincarnation and karma, that are offered to human beings.

And that is the archangel that breaks everything apart so that it can be renewed; that levels everything out so that it can be rebuilt and recreated socially – but from within. That is Michael, under whose leadership we can stand if it is our will to do so. And that is what it depends on.

An Experience of Music and Destiny, Advent 1954

Introductory words by the editor

Choosing examples of Karl König's presentations for Advent and Christmas was not easy because for almost every year of his life since the move to Camphill, he gave a series of lectures on specific themes or aspects of Christmas that began with the first Sunday of Advent and included at least five lectures and shorter addresses (usually including a short address for the New Year) until the day of the Three Kings' celebration on January 6. As often happens when faced with difficult decisions, something unexpected turned up. We were able to identify, through entries in König's diary for 1954, notes that we had previously seen but had not connected with a lecture: they seemed to be more an unusual musical study.

Suddenly the situation of Advent 1954 became significant. It was at that time that König realised he was seriously ill and, as a result of medical advice, withdrew almost completely from life in Camphill. He was faced with the prospect of no longer being able to travel and lecture or continue his therapeutic work, as well handing over all his duties and administrative tasks in the growing community and movement. This restriction lasted throughout most of 1955 until he decided, in December of that year, to return to work regardless. He was internationally active for the next ten years until his death at Easter in 1966.

Excerpts from König's diary of 1954 can serve as an introduction to the following, rather enigmatic notes, which have been translated and transcribed in hand-writing so as to come close to their original form (translations by the editor). In the week before Advent, König had travelled to southern England to give two courses and a public lecture in Hawkwood College. For Advent he was then in the Camphill Schools Community, Thornbury:

Sunday, November 28, 1954

In the morning I admit the children to the Sunday Service that Tilla holds. They are very well-behaved and reverent. The Advent Garden is in the afternoon, and I am just as moved to the heart as I was 27 years ago when I experienced it for the first time in the Sonnenhof in Arlesheim; that was the moment when I was led to devoting myself to Curative Education. Afterwards I prepared myself for the evening lecture and gradually everything grows and flows together that I want to say. However, with this I suddenly experience something completely new to me: it is as though music flowed around me and the rhythm of the lecture sounds through the flow as if a symphony was unfolding itself, or a sonata in four movements. And it feels as though every lecture should be composed of four parts in order to be correct; that is one of the secrets of the art of lecturing.

Terrible pains in the chest prevent the lecture from being as good as I had hoped.

Despite seeing about twenty of the new children in his surgery, holding a Class Lesson, and giving advice to a number of co-workers in various private conversations, he noted down on the evening of Monday, November 29:

> Then, however, I am more than tired and the cramp attacks have increased; often they become almost unbearable. Now I begin to grasp that it is angina pectoris.

After further work in a very full schedule in London, König decided to go to a doctor on December 2:

> Dr Shirley-Smith did an ECG that showed coronary damage, and indeed angina pectoris was diagnosed. I was told I was not to work at all for at least three weeks … In a way it is a relief because by now I feel that I am at the end of my energy.
>
> In the evening I go to a concert. Klemperer conducts and first Marcia funèbre from Eroica is played in honour of Furtwangler who has just died. And I have to wonder: 'Is this also in my honour?'

The following evening, Friday December 3, he wrote:

> The night ended at about 4am due to a series of chest cramps and only with the greatest effort am I able to get up. Now the word 'angina pectoris' has sounded, everything seems to have a different acoustic colour, also all the pain and fits of cramp that I have already had to suffer.
>
> Now I remember also that it was the first Saturday in December, 7 years ago in this very room, that I had my first bad fit of cramp.

An Advent-Sonata.

28. November 1954
1st Advent Sunday

I. Movement
Introduction: Grave

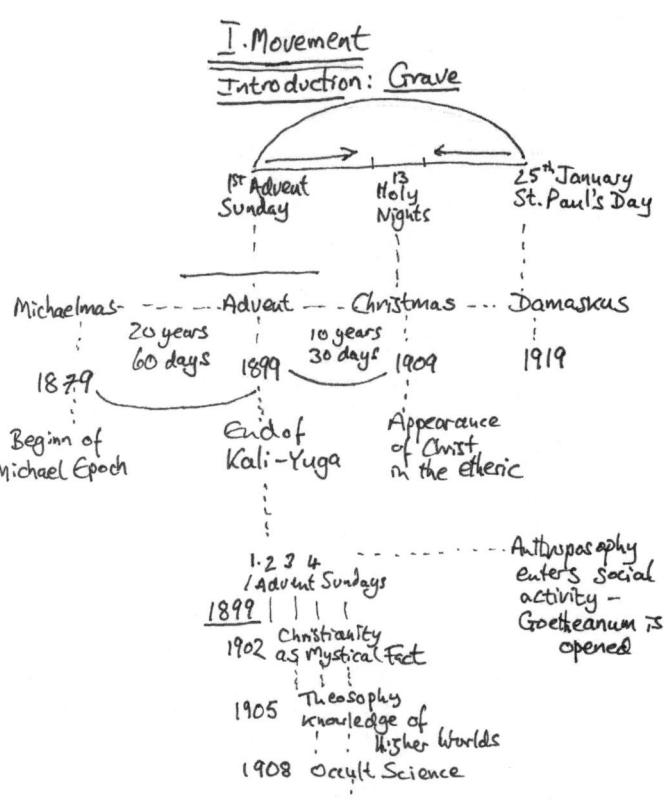

II. Movement
Andante Sostenuto

The loss of festivals.

Easter is in Russia
Christmas in Central Europe
The West has no specific festival

This loss belongs to changes in the whole of humanity. The old fourfold structure is now through 1879, 1899 + 1909 threefold [it was Africa, Asia, Europe, America]

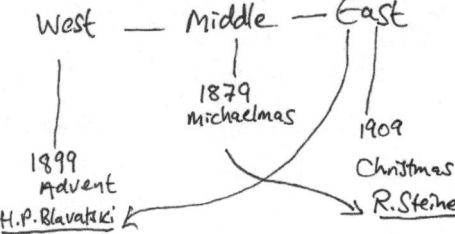

III^d Movement

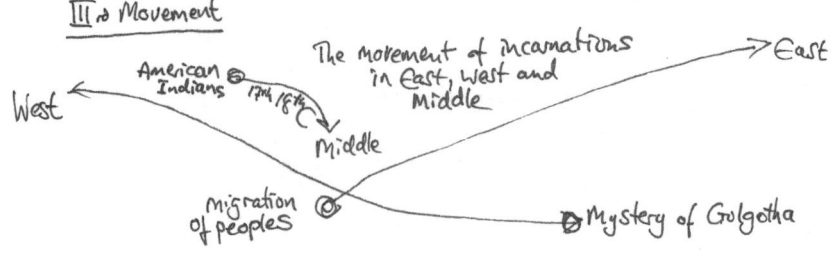

IVth Movement

Allegro alla marcia

Out of the various movements and migration the situation of our time has developed

1). West ← Middle
   From the Middle Michaelic thinking must re-enliven the dead thoughts of the West

   Michaelmas

   Through this Advent can come

2). West ← From the west the light of the end of Kali-Yuga must begin to ray out to the East. Then Christmas can arise there and an understanding for the appearance of Christ in the etheric will awaken. → East

3). Then Earth will shine out in its threefold way

Advent	Michaelmas	Christmas
Death and resurrection	Transfiguration	Birth of Spirit-Light in the darkness

Today it is still so that in
　　Middle Europe　Christmas
　in Russia　　Easter
are essential parts of society
Nationalism has destroyed Christmas
Bolshevism has driven out Easter
What can the West celebrate?
The middle needs to bring Advent to the West
Then a new Christmas festival will ray out from
the West to the East. In the middle, however,
a new Michaelmas festival will arise.

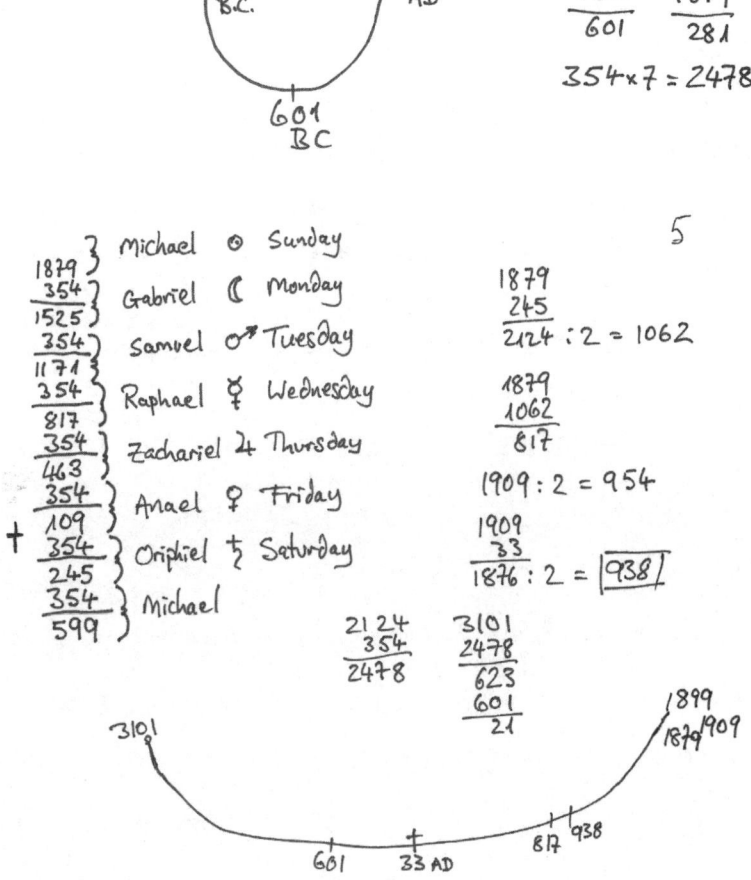

Michaelmas 1879
| . . . . . . 60 days . . . . 20 years
Advent 1899   30 years
| . . . . 30 days . . . . 10 years
Christmas 1909

1 year = 3 days
2⅓ years = 7 days = | 1 week |
30 years = 90 days = | 13 weeks | = a season

Beginn of
Passiontide . . . . . . Michaelmas
Ostern . . . . Advent
Ascension . . . . . Christmas
Whitsun . . . . . 6th January

    1st Advent Sunday . . . 1899 . . . . end of Kali-Yuga
    2nd Advent Sunday . . . 1902 . . . . Christianity as
                                                              Mystical Fact
    3rd Advent Sunday . . . . 1905 . . . . Theosophie
                                                               Knowledge of H. Worlds
    4th Advent Sunday . . . . 1908 . . . Occult Science
    Christmas . . . . . . 1909 . . . . Gospel of St. Luke
                                             |
                                          5th Gospel

Notes from Karl König's diary for his lecture An Experience of Music and Destiny, *given during Advent, 1954.*

On the Significance of the Twelve Holy Days

Lecture given on December 13, 1944

Already in primeval times people felt that the days and nights of the winter solstice are special ones. During this time, which follows the lowest position of the midday sun with regard to the Earth, the human soul went through certain experiences that were only possible during this particular part of the year.

Ancient people knew that during these days and nights their soul had certain experiences they never had at any other time of the year. The inner ear was opened and they could understand what the animals were saying. The language of cows and birds, of horses and hens, was distinguished by them. And those who were able to listen more carefully could also hear the songs and melodies of the seeds in the dark earth. They could hear how the world powers of music were streaming down from heaven. This is actually the time when in the first hallowed night the shepherds were able to hear the song of the heavenly host, the voice of the angels proclaiming the birth of Jesus.

Long before the first holy night this song could be heard. In the mysteries of ancient times, and especially in those mysteries that were conducted by the priests who called themselves Druids, the winter solstice was a very special time. The darkness of winter and the cold, hard earth created within their souls a disposition that led them to experience that which is expressed in the phrase: seeing the sun at midnight. The outer light had disappeared, bare and barren was the earthly womb, nature was silent, life was darkened. Within the soul, however, the word could be heard:

> The sun his ancient hymn of wonder
> Is pouring out to kindred spheres.[1]

The sun resounded to the ears of the soul and the year began its new cycle. From this moment on the seeds started to grow, life was awakened anew, and the sprouting and quickened rhythms of growth started again to shed their blessing upon the earth.

Is there any reality to all this ancient belief? Is there any need for the modern individual to reflect on these old observations? Is it still possible to wake up to this World-Sphere in which the souls of older generations dwelt during the time of the thirteen holy nights? And what are these holy nights?

In the rest of continental Europe, and even on this island, some people, particularly older farmers, still watch the weather very carefully during these thirteen holy nights. They study the strength of the wind, the colour of dawn and dusk, the amount of snow and rain, and they write all this down with hands heavy from work. The old farmers know that the weather during these nights and days predicts the weather of the following year. They believe that each of these twelve consecutive days indicates the weather of the consecutive months. Is the world of all the elements nearer to human beings during this season of the year? Can human beings communicate in a more inner and serious way with all that happens 'behind the curtain' of sense appearance?

ON THE SIGNIFICANCE OF THE TWELVE HOLY DAYS

The twelve holy days and thirteen holy nights last from December 24 to January 6; New Year's Eve lies exactly in the middle of this time. If we mark these days and nights on a line it looks like the following drawing:

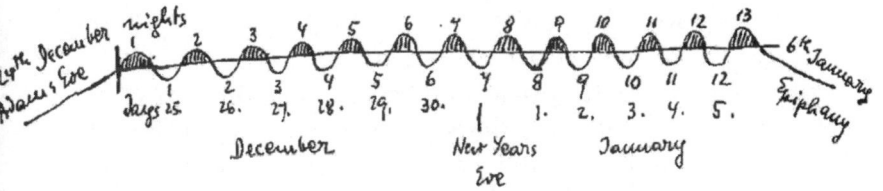

Drawing showing 'holy days' and holy nights from Christmas Eve to Epiphany.

The night that follows Christmas Eve is the first of the holy nights. The night that precedes the day of Epiphany, the day of the three Wise Men, is the last of these holy nights. Enclosed by these nights are the twelve days, of which the first one is Christmas Day, the last one January 5.

If we want to try and understand this time in a proper way we have to ask ourselves: why are there twelve days, and why are they ordered between two such significant days as December 24, Adam and Eve's Day, and January 6, the day of Epiphany? This period is roughly a thirtieth part of a whole year, and if we take this time as indicated – as twelve days and thirteen nights – it is exactly a thirtieth of the 365 days that build up a whole year.

We know that the planet Saturn takes thirty years to orbit the sun, and it is easy to understand that the mathematical relation between the revolution of Saturn around the sun is exactly the same as the one between the time of the holy nights and the solar year itself. We can express this in the following way:

Saturn : sun = sun : holy nights
30 : 1 = 1 : 1/30

This is now an interesting statement as it shows to us that the time of the holy nights is, in its temporal aspects, directly connected with the sun and Saturn. One should learn to look again beyond the pure arithmetic of such statements. They indicate more; they lead on to throw some light onto what actually happens.

The twelve holy days are like a gateway through which the human soul can connect itself with the sphere of Saturn. Rudolf Steiner has told us that it is Saturn, the outermost of the ancient planets, which carries the memory of the whole cosmos. Saturn is like a registrar who puts down all that happened during the evolution of our earthly system. People whose souls are prepared to realise these world-memories can find an open gate during the thirteen holy nights into the Book of the World, the sphere of the planet Saturn.

The number of the twelve days is still significant in another way in connection to a certain cosmic cycle. The planet Jupiter takes roughly twelve years to orbit the sun. The exact time is 4,332 days. If we divide this number by the number of days in a solar year we get twelve. This means that an ordinary day of the common sun year is equivalent to twelve Jupiter-days. As Jupiter needs twelve times as much time to orbit the sun as the earth, the twelve holy days are equivalent to one Jupiter-day. This again can be expressed in the following way:

$$1 \text{ year} : 1 \text{ day} = 12 \text{ years} : 12 \text{ days}$$
$$1 \text{ solar year} : 1 \text{ solar day} = 1 \text{ Jupiter-year} : \text{Jupiter-day}$$

The twelve holy days are therefore equivalent to one Jupiter-day. And here we reach another significant statement. The arithmetical statement has again to be seen in a larger context than the simple, isolated fact itself. It expresses the significant truth that during the time of the holy nights, the human soul is able to live in the sphere of Jupiter. It is not so that any random accumulation of twelve odd days express a Jupiter-day. It is just between Christmas and Epiphany that the true and real Jupiter-day falls together with the ordinary twelve days or thirteen nights of this holy time of the year. If the smaller circle of the drawing here would indicate the earthly year and the bigger circle the Jovian year, then these circles can express more than a sign but a symbol of the Earth-sphere and Jupiter-sphere, and we are able to see the following:

Drawing indicating the earthly year (small circle) and the Jovian year (large circle)

During the time of the holy nights the Jupiter–sphere and the Earth-sphere are penetrating each other. The cosmic realm of Jupiter unites itself very closely with the earthly realm. If we remember now that Rudolf Steiner indicated to us that the orbit of Jupiter circumscribes the sphere which once upon a time the earth occupied during its Old Sun evolution, we will understand the saying of the Druid priests: seeing the sun at midnight. It is the old and hidden sphere of the Old Sun evolution that penetrates into earthly space. One Jupiter day, so to speak, is given to humanity on earth every year; this is the time of the holy nights.

If we consider the year (and each year with the same amount of days) consisting of 360 days, the true Jupiter-year needs 360 earthly years to be fulfilled. That means 360 holy night-times have to be added together to make up a cosmic Jupiter-year and this is 360 earthly years. Of these 360 years the actual Jupiter year, which is commonly counted as twelve years, makes a thirtieth part. This is the same part the twelve holy nights make of the year, and the same part the whole year makes of the Saturn-year. Here we see how interwoven these cosmic rhythms are and how the holy nights are a centre for this tapestry of cosmic and earthly relationship. The threads of Jupiter, Saturn, sun and earth meet each other and penetrate each other during this blessed time.

The whole of earthly nature is directly influenced during this time by the cosmic forces of Saturn and Jupiter. The memories of world evolution print their sign and pattern into the world of matter. The forces of archetypal images that once upon a time permeated the whole of creation are now instilled into the earth during the time of the holy nights as forces of creative memory.

Jupiter has always been connected with the forces that still show their influence on the earth, although they are ever-changing. They express themselves in all that constitutes our weather. As Zeus these forces were seen to throw lightning into the world; his wrath commanded the thunder, and it was he who urged the wind and the rain to pour down on earth and drown the people who did not listen to his commands. It is the power of the Ancient Sun world that still acts in all that we experience around us as weather. There the elementary forces are still alive, working and creating. That is really why the farmer sits down and observes the weather during this holy time, because the Jupiter-day between Christmas and Epiphany is the well-spring of the weather for the following year. If we draw the holy nights as a circle and the following year around them, like the flower around the calyx, we can easily see the connection between the days of this holy time and the months of the year that follow.

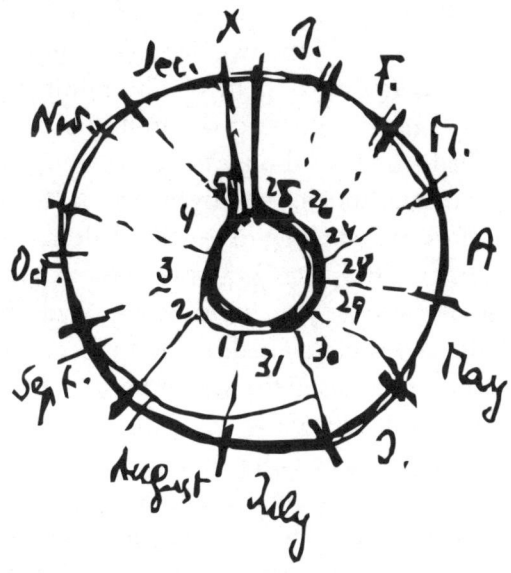

Drawing showing the holy nights as a circle within a larger circle representing the following year.

Then we see how New Year's Eve corresponds to the change from July to August, the time during which the seeds that are impregnated during the New Year's night ripen. Those are two consecutive months, by the way, that have thirty-one days.

It is also of great significance that the time of the twelve holy days reaches from one year into another. This is more than just a link. On the tree of time each year ripens from January to December. The bud develops from January to March, the blossom opens at Easter and withers away during Pentecost, then the fruit starts to ripen, but in the growing fruit the seed for the new plant is already hidden. The twelve holy days are the seed that springs from the old plant to create the new one. Seven days, from December 25 to 31, build up the part of the seed that still belongs to the old plant. Then there are five days, from January 1 to 5. The seed consists then of seven and five days: the seven days of the old year and the five days of the new one. This is significant as it throws light on the number of loaves with which Christ could feed the multitude. With seven loaves he feeds the four thousand, those who belonged to the fourth cultural epoch; with five loaves he feeds the five thousand, those who belong to the fifth cultural epoch (the current epoch). The seven loaves of the old year and the five loaves of the new year build up the seed of the holy nights. This seed is penetrated by the Jupiter- and Saturn-forces. These forces make the seed grow into the new year through which our life guides us.

Two pillars stand at either end of this seed of time: the Adam and Eve Day and Epiphany. Old wisdom knew why those names had to be given to those days. Adam and Eve represent the old creation; Epiphany marks the day Christ is born into the body of Jesus – this is the day of the Baptism in the River Jordan. The new time had come, and the new creation was laid as a seed into the decaying fruit of the old world.

In between the old cycle and the new cycle of human and earthly existence there rests the time of the holy nights. Like a jewel it is set into the ring of the year. May this precious stone be more and more beheld by the growing conscience of our time.

New Year's Eve Address, 1965–66

Camphill Hall, Scotland

Again we stand in the middle of the twelve holy nights, the most exalted period of the whole year, which one can experience as being so very special. And at the centre of this period is this very hour in which the past year moves into the new one. We may experience this central part like a peak, or also like the deepest depth. In such a moment heights and depths are one because time stands still. In the stillness of time, in this hollow but peaceful space of existence, each of us can turn to ourselves, looking backwards and forwards. At the same time one should look upwards in order to listen to the voice with which the heavens speak to us. We can also say that the heavens speak with a script, and if we learn to read this script then we can also hear it, and when we hear it, we can imagine it like a song, a melody. It is a melody wherein the words and phrases speak to human beings on earth, to let us know what we should perceive in this very hour.

If we would look out now, we would see the moon setting in the west. It is a half-moon, shining with a bright light. And somewhere just below the horizon there is the sun, and the sun is accompanied to the east by Mercury, to the west by Mars and Venus, and these two are very close together. Between this pair and the moon we can imagine

Saturn, below and behind us. Almost opposite to Saturn, although not exactly, is Jupiter in all its brightness, shining down on earth. So Jupiter is the only planet that is visible at the moment, besides the setting moon. Perhaps we can try to imagine this picture so that we can have a glimpse at the script that heaven reveals to us at this moment.

What could it be that this script is saying to us?

Mercury stands at about the same place at which it stood last year at this very hour, although a year ago it was all totally different. The moon was close to Mercury, yet a few hours before the beginning of the new year – the year which is now closing – the moon had completely eclipsed Mercury; Venus stood next to it, watching, as it were, the interplay between Mercury and the moon. And we can remember that just in this hour Mars was rising in the east, standing in the twenty-third degree of the Virgin, thereby indicating a very special place in the whole of the zodiac. This position of Mars in the constellation of the Virgin reminded us of the great event that occurred on Mars 360 years ago, in 1604.[1] And it was this image, this healing power that accompanied us throughout this year. We again turn to Mercury at this time of year, but now the setting moon and Mercury form a straight line, which is part of a huge cosmic triangle shining through space. One point of this triangle is indicated by Mercury, the second by the moon, and the peak of the triangle points into the constellation of the Lion, the heart of the universe. This is the great image that begins to speak to us in this very hour, introducing the year 1966. If we try to understand what this triangle means, we will hear the voice, the melody of Jupiter. We learn to understand that during this year and also next year, Jupiter will move very steadily, gradually, step by step, in the direction in which this triangle points. Jupiter, with the voice of the Kyrios, reaches out to approach the sign of the Lion – the constellation of the cosmic heart.

NEW YEAR'S EVE ADDRESS, 1965–66

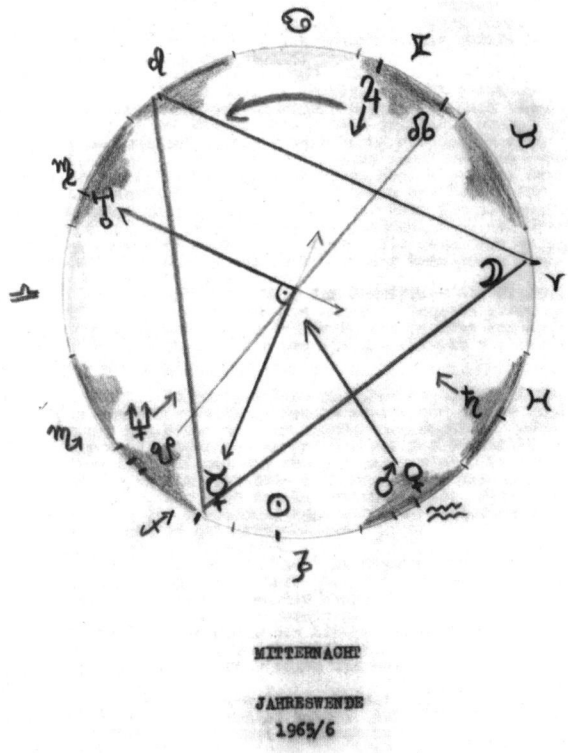

New Year star chart.

If we turn our understanding to this, we will also remember that it is now 33 years since the beginning of the events in Middle Europe that led to the destruction of Germany and large parts of the world. We will remember that 33 years ago the Beast appeared out of the depths and started to slay everything that wanted to be filled with a certain amount of goodwill. Whoever is not willing to see this must remain blind and dumb for everything that happens in the world today, because what started in 1933 brought about the chaos in which we have to live now and will still have to live in the years to come. What happened then was meant to veil, to destroy, something else that happened at the same time. To this I still want to refer. You see, the triangle and the melody of Kyrios-Jupiter, and that reaching out towards the sign of the Lion, want to remind us and strengthen our belief for the other event that happened in 1933. The being of Christ began to appear within the whole etheric sphere of the Earth. Two thousand years ago, at the event of the Transfiguration, he was already beheld by his three disciples, Peter, James and John. In the same way he now started to shine in the light of the Transfiguration. He began to walk near individual human beings or appeared among groups of people when they were suffering, when they were in despair, or when they had lost their faith. At such times he came to be with them, to be the Comforter and the Healer. Though only very few could experience him to begin with, a few more began to know this new Christ event. It has occurred over the course of 33 years, at the same time that chaos, decay and destruction have spread ever wider. It is still a small light, but it is the light of hope and faith and love.

And whenever we look up during the course of the nights of January, February and March,[2] and then again towards the coming autumn and winter of this year, and we behold the light of Jupiter, let us remember that Jupiter sings the song of the Kyrios-Christ, the Kyrios-Christ who has appeared and will appear more and more strongly as the Comforter and the Healer of human beings and of humanity. To prepare ourselves for this so that we might become aware of it, we should remember that the one who revealed all this to us is Rudolf Steiner. To renew this knowledge daily in faith, hope and love, we close the old year and enter the new one speaking the words of the Foundation Stone, which is the preparatory word – the preparatory song – for the human heart to be able to perceive this ever-growing light of the Christ.[3]

The 'Entry into Jerusalem'

(Adapted from Mark, Chapter 11)

Two disciples are sent out
To find the donkey foal
That awaits the Lord
In the settlement
Ahead of them.

The donkey's foal is the new wisdom
Which is given to the two disciples
From out of the moon's Horn of Plenty.
In the moon sphere of the settlement
The wise men of humanity's ancient past,
The seven Holy Rishis, wait
To pass on this donkey's foal.

It is no longer ancient wisdom of the moon,
Shining once more to Earth.
The foal is the new crescent moon
Laden with the lunar disc.
The image of the Grail
Enters now into the City of Death.

Jerusalem,
You City of Death,
With Hosanna you now receive
The Grail's light
Of new thinking.

Jerusalem,
You City of Death,
Oh human head,
Oh human brain,
Receive the light of Christ
In the glow of new thought.

Waves of knowledge and wisdom
Once rayed out
From the full lunar globe
Down into human heads.
Thoughts of World-Spirit
Flowed toward
Humanity's being.

But now the sun-globe's light
Sails on the boat of the moon
Into earthly spheres
And three times Christ Jesus enters
Jerusalem,
The City of Death.

The first time he rides
On the donkey's foal.
People see him
As the Messiah
And call Hosanna
With light of heart.

Hosanna rays out
From their hearts
To all the widths of space,
It flows to the heavens
And leaves the Earth behind.
The second time,

THE 'ENTRY INTO JERUSALEM'

Before reaching the City,
He curses first the fig tree.
It no longer carries fruits
For the old wisdom has died;
In him new homeland has arisen.
The force of new wisdom
Can now purge the temple of the head,
Disperse all changers of earthly thought,
All buyers and sellers
Of wisdom obsolete,
The dove dealers
Of faded mysteries
Out from the treasury of the brain;
Mercilessly.

The fig tree withers.
Ancient wisdom has died.
In its place, however,
The seed of faith is planted
In the centre of the head.
But that new faith
Is from now on
A shining star
On each forehead.
And new faith can live
In each word
Of prayer fulfilled.

And for a third time
Christ makes his entry
Into this City of Death,
Jerusalem.
The scribes in the temple ask
Out of what source
He performs his deeds.

But he tells them:
If you do not know it
Out of yourself and your beliefs,
Then nowhere will you find
The written proof.

For the first entry
Human steps are born
From out the 'I'.

For the second entrance
The human word
Is created from the forces
Of the fulfilled 'I'.

For the third entry
Human thinking is brought
To the sharp cutting edge
Of conscience.

The head of wisdom past
Is destroyed.
Ancient knowledge, prior content,
Becomes now transformed
As vessel for a head renewed.
This new head is now
The first temple of the Grail
To be built in Earth's
Ether space.

Now the Light-Temple
Can shine
Through moon's spheres.
The cupola of light
Awakens

On the light-ray pillars.
The temple builds itself
Sublimely
In spirit's coloured flow.
New wisdom
Becomes the chalice
The Lord's blood
To now receive.

The Experience of Easter Within the Human Being

Notes for a lecture on Easter Sunday, April 18, 1954

When we human beings try to come nearer to the Christian festivals, the experiences of the festivals can grow to be more significant; they grow more intimate also. We grow in our experiences because we gradually get a feeling for the living spiritual being that stands behind each of the Christian festivals. We meet that being from different sides and different aspects. Each year it can show us another face. Sometimes you can experience an illuminated face; other times a face full of sorrow or sometimes the being does not look at us at all. In gradually recognising the spiritual beings behind the festivals, we are like children who start to wake up. We only wake up if we are really honest with regard to our experiences. We must be clean when entering the door of a festival.

There is a threefold experience of Easter:

1. We can look at nature around us. Winter has come to an end, the hard earth is softened by the coming spring. This way of experiencing Easter is not Christian, but heathen. The agnostics say that at the tuning point of the sun the earth is resurrected. But this refers only to a change of life phase, not the resurrection.

2. When beholding the living power of nature, we can experience a radiating joy, like it can be experienced in the scene that takes place on Easter morning in Goethe's *Faust*.[1] But this is also not fundamentally a Christian experience, the human being does not meet the Christ on this path. All this still belongs to pre-Christian times. The mysteries of Adonis were connected with the experience of joy within the human soul. From these sources our souls may in future be led to the true experience of resurrection.

3. The spiritual experience of Easter lives within the human being in the faculty of being able to learn, understand, and bring order in the world surrounding us (nature, humanity, stars, history, etc.). We must learn not only to see and accept the world, but must learn to look behind it, in order to recognise the working of the heavenly, divine powers! Only by means of this faculty we can come nearer to the true experience of Easter.

What altogether do we know about Easter, the resurrection, about the Christ? What do we really know in spite of all that Dr Steiner gave to humanity? We can have feelings and thoughts about the Easter events. We can learn about Christ, but did we ever experience Christ from I to I? Easter actually means to meet the Christ! In order to go towards this aim there are two possibilities:

1. In studying the gospels and beholding the images given in the gospels – also by studying the experiences of saints and mystics – we also learn more intimately about the Christ. Anna Katharina Emmerick describes intensively the Easter events and other facts connected with Christ's being on Earth. Through such descriptions our hearts may be deeply moved and feeling will move in us, but honestly we do not meet the Christ.

2. We can first also learn from Rudolf Steiner and the Church Fathers about the Christ, how he descended step by step until the Baptism in the Jordan took place. We can try to imagine and think of all this.

But where in this is the immediate experience of the Christ himself?

When we once learn to know our own inability to meet the Christ, when we experience this tremendous lameness, then is achieved the first step to meeting the Christ. This experience of lameness must be felt in the depth of our soul.

We must get to know the human being in order to understand the great battle to meet the Christ. Let us follow the development of the human being until twenty-one years of age. In the first three years we learn to walk, to talk and to think. At three years we say 'I' to ourselves. In this moment we know, 'I am I'. This we will not lose until the moment of death. However, at the age of three we are not really ready for this great experience.

1. Up to the 7th year the human being develops in the physical realm.

2. 7th–14th year: living powers unfold.

3. 14th–21st year: the forces of the soul start to unfold.

4. From 21st year onwards the human being is ready to be a carrier of their own ego-existence.

The fulfilment of the third year really only comes about when we are twenty-one years old, only then can we actually say, 'I am I'. Between the third and the twenty-first years is quite an abyss. In the original plan of creation it was meant to happen in the following way:

1. From the 3rd year onwards the child lives only in imitation.

2. 7th–14th year: the child should be led only by authority without being already self-conscious.

3. 14th–21st year: the young person should fill their soul with dreams of their ideas.

4. Only with the 21st year should the awareness 'I am I' enter us (not at all after the first three years).

That the development of human consciousness has become different from what is described here is the result of the Fall. After three years we are in bodily existence, but we are not at all ready for the I-experience.

This great gap between the third and twenty-first year caused death, illness and malformation. Humanity left Paradise too early. When saying 'I' to ourselves at three years of age, we repeat the Fall.

Where does this inability to meet the Christ come from? It lies within the great abyss. Humanity has to overcome this gap. That we become able to do so is only possible because Christ came himself. He came in order to heal this gap. But what can we as individual human beings really do towards the overcoming of this gap? Angelus Silesius said: 'The Cross we can only redeem, when we erect it in us every hour.'[2]

In earlier times some people withdrew three days before Easter in continuous meditation and contemplation. For instance, Karl IV had a special room, a cell, built only for him in his castle, solely in order to retire for these days.³

To do this in the same way would not be right any more for today's human beings. But we can do this by withdrawing into the realm of thinking, because we are able to control our thoughts. In this way we can prepare ourselves for Easter.

Maundy Thursday

We can prepare the Upper Room. We can do this in the realm of thinking. All the experiences throughout the last year shall be gathered in thought in order to prepare the Upper Room. That which is gathered must be ordered quite clearly. Nothing shall disturb this order. Then we can set out to meet with our thinking and try to understand the ordered experiences of the past year. In doing so we enter:

Good Friday

In spite of all that we achieved on the day before ordering and gathering, we do not experience the reality that stands behind all that. Not to be able to find the reality, not to know why I am on this earth, causes pain and utter despair. In the end I am so much in despair that I cannot stand it any more and question the sense of living and the possibility of achieving anything.

Saturday

Out of this darkness something new is now gained. I have given up pondering why it all is and try to be as calm as possible within my soul.

Easter Morning

All ordered thoughts burst asunder like the stone rolled away on Easter morning. Out of this rises a new understanding, which is given to humanity out of grace. In the recognition of this grace, the first sight of Christ will be experienced directly.

In this preparation for Easter, which means to try to overcome our lameness, we can become able to meet the Christ. Humanity today must break asunder its own tomb. Only a renewed effort can bring us to the real Easter experience. True thinking in images must arise – living thought. Easter is not only a joyful experience, it is something of a more intimate nature within the human soul and spirit. Only if we sacrifice our own thinking can cosmic communion be achieved. Human and World thoughts must meet.

World Breath and World Pulse

Lecture given on Palm Sunday, April 11, 1965.

The lectures I have decided to give this Easter will have a quite definite subject. An overall title for them could be: 'World Pulse and World Breath', a vast theme of which I hope I am able to convey a few aspects. Let us begin our deliberations today, on Palm Sunday, the day that opens Holy Week. Today the Passion begins, and in each one of us those world images arise that were inscribed into the Earth and the human soul when, two thousand years ago, the Mystery of Golgotha took place. It was as if during the seven days from Palm Sunday to Easter Sunday something happened that was like the point of balance, the ego point, of all Earth existence. In reality we can only imagine this correctly if we realise that the eyes of the hierarchies and of all creation – the eyes of the universe, so to speak – gazed upon Jerusalem and Bethany, which were at the centre of these events. It was as if the world stood still: the world breath stopped; the world heartbeat ceased. It was as if seven 'world minutes' passed in complete silence, and in that silence tiny seeds began to sprout – but tiny only from the point of view of the world, which continued growing and radiating a power of life throughout the centuries.

During Holy Week world images arose that have accompanied humanity ever since: Christ entering Jerusalem on the ass; Christ casting the money-changers out of the Temple; Christ in the circle of his disciples cursing the fig tree; Christ on the Mount of Olives relating the apocalypse to his disciples, revealing to them vision after vision of the future; Christ being anointed by Mary Magdalene before his death. Image follows image: the last supper, the garden of Gethsemane, the capture, the judgment, the walk to Golgotha, the crucifixion, the burial, the women going to the tomb during Easter night, the event of the resurrection. Then follow three appearances of the resurrected Christ: first to Mary Magdalene on Easter Sunday, then to the two disciples on the road to Emmaus, and in the evening to the whole circle of the disciples. These are images that continually accompany the human soul if it tries to enter the coming days of Holy Week with a believing and awakened consciousness. Indeed, these are events in every human soul, provided that it is willing to make them conscious by bringing them to mind each day, even if only for a short while, whether in the evening or the morning, trying to imagine Jerusalem and Bethany and, gropingly perhaps, striving to behold what happened at that time.

By doing this we may also remember that a new year is now beginning. In fact, Holy Week is the last week of the previous year, which began on Easter Sunday and took its course through the circle of the past twelve months. In Holy Week the year draws to a close and on Easter morning it starts anew. Nowadays, we celebrate the beginning of a new year in January, but in previous ages it was celebrated at a variety of times. For instance, in the third post-Atlantean epoch the year began at midsummer, not only in Egypt and Babylon, but in all those regions where the high culture of the Druids spread in all its dignified magnificence. In those days when the light of the sun began to decrease they experienced that something new developed within the human soul on Earth.

Later, from the earliest beginnings of the influence of

Judaism, the peoples of the Middle East celebrated new year at Michaelmas; and even to the present day the Jewish year begins with the harvest. When the corn was harvested they sensed that a new year was beginning, and they tried to experience their own rising power of thought and ego together with the waning sun. At that time Michael was known as the countenance of Yahweh (today we refer to him as the countenance of Christ).

Later still, when Christ was born at Christmas, the beginning of the year was celebrated on December 25, and this practice continued into the Middle Ages until, with the introduction of the Gregorian calendar, it was moved to the first day of January. Just as in primeval times, so nowadays there is a repetition of change. Gradually we may begin to feel that in our time the year should really begin on Easter Sunday, and that this particular day should be celebrated as the true beginning of the year.

This is the real reason behind the struggle for the introduction of a fixed Easter, because a date fixed by human beings according to earthly considerations is in reality the opposite of what is needed, namely the emergence of Easter as a new time to begin the year. The truth is that the breath of a new year begins with the day of resurrection, and it is the shadow of this event that really compels us to battle for the preservation of Easter as a festival directed by the cosmos.

Perhaps some of you may remember the passage in Goethe's *Faust* in which Faust tries to explain this to Wagner during their so-called 'Easter walk' when he says:

> Released from ice are brook and river
> By the quickening glance of the gracious spring
> The colours of hope to the valley cling
> And weak old winter himself must shiver
> Withdrawn to the mountains, crownless king:
> Whence, still retreating, he sends again

> Impotent showers of sleet that darken
> In belts across the green o' the plain.
> But the sun will permit no white to sparkle;
> Every form in development moveth;
> He will brighten the world with the tints he loveth.[1]

In these words Goethe describes what we all experience at this time of year. The ice crust of the earth has melted and a breathing out begins that leads all the developing, sprouting growth from the depths of the earth into the fullness of nature. But, as Rudolf Steiner has pointed out, this breath exhales only from the earth and by itself could never bring forth the Easter that strives to emerge, for this breath has to be met by another.

Let us turn to the *Calendar of the Soul* and with its help try to understand some of the secrets of existence. The first verse, the verse of Easter week, which starts on Easter Sunday irrespective of the actual date on which Easter falls, begins with the following words:

> When from out the worlds of space
> The sun speaks to human sense.

This means that two streams of breath begin to meet. Rising from the human being and from the earth there is the stream of earthly breath, towards which a cosmic breath streams from the cosmos. This is meant quite concretely, and later I will explain what it means. It is the breathing of the year, the meeting and release of these two breathing processes, which begins at Easter. One breathing process ascends from the earth, the other descends from the cosmos, both meet and begin to interpenetrate. They unite and intermingle completely at St John's tide, when the world breath kisses the earth breath. Thereafter they begin to separate further and further from each other through the following weeks and months, until in autumn the world breath again returns to the heights and the earth breath enters the depths. At Christmas they are furthest apart, being completely separated from each other. Over the course of winter, during January, February and March, they strive towards each other again in order to meet at Easter. During Holy Week we are at the end of the world-year of breath. Earth breath and world breath join hands in order to gradually come near to each other.

Now listen to the last verse of the *Calendar of the Soul*, which is used from Palm Sunday onwards:

> When from depths of soul
> The spirit turns to world existence

This is the verse for the present week. We should turn to it every day and ask ourselves: what does 'spirit' mean here? These lines point to the breathing process. However, this is only part of the answer, because a response immediately resounds from outside:

> And beauty gushes from the widths of space

We should try to experience the reality of 'beauty gush[ing] from the widths of space'. Then we are told what is behind this beautiful sheen:

> Then out from farthest heavens
> The force of life draws into human forms
> And, working powerfully, unites
> The spirit's being with the human being.

This is the mutual breathing process that takes place and which opens up the world year out of the depths of the soul. Out of the depths of the Earth the spirit turns to world existence. From the world existence an answer is given, for from the gushing beauty that we meet comes the force of life out of the cosmos, which, working powerfully, unites the spirit's being with the human being.

The question now arises which, if we take the *Calendar of the Soul* literally and try to understand it, really is a profound question: what is this force of life, which 'out from farthest heavens... draws into human forms'? Is it just a phrase or is it much more than words? Is it a living activity? Let us study the verses for Passiontide and those of the weeks leading up to Passiontide once more. In them a very special word is used in two places in the original German, a word that was in fact created by Rudolf Steiner and which therefore demands our particular attention as to its meaning. The word is *Werdelust*, meaning 'rapture of becoming'.

When Carnival week is over and Lent begins, verse 47 of the *Calendar of the Soul* says:

> Now rapture of becoming would arise
> From out the lap of worlds
> Quickening the senses' glory.

Then something is told about the human being:

> May it find my thinking's might
> Well-armed by powers divine,
> Which strongly live within my inner being.

Several renderings of this unusual word exist in different translations. The reader may wish to compare these with the form used here.[2] For the present let us ponder the first three lines:

> Now rapture of becoming would arise

> From out the lap of worlds
> Quickening the senses' glory.

The soul divines that 'Carnival' (meaning 'farewell to the flesh') has passed, and something new is beginning. In the 'lap of worlds' the process of development begins to move and in it be heard the budding 'rapture of becoming'. *Werdelust* appears again three weeks later in the verse for the second week of Lent, but then in an entirely different context:

> Now speaks unto the human I,
> Mightily revealing
> And setting free its being's force
> The world-being's rapture of becoming.

Here the 'rapture of becoming' is no longer in the 'lap of worlds' but is beginning to resound of itself. In this instance, three weeks later than the first, the heavens have opened and the 'rapture of becoming' appears and begins to exchange words with the human I. The 'rapture of becoming' says:

> Bearing my life into thee
> Out of the spell of its enchantment
> I shall attain my own true goal.

This is a meeting of active powers, a meeting of the human I and the world being's 'rapture of becoming'. But what does this really mean?

A conversation develops in which the embracing world breath, which begins to join hands with the earth breath, turns to the human I. But is this world breath, this 'rapture of becoming' that arises out of the 'lap of worlds', the same as the world I? We know that there are verses in the

Calendar of the Soul that are related to each other as polar opposites, for instance verses 52 and 1, and verses 51 and 2, and that these polarities, as far as I understand them, express universal laws.

We may now wonder whether the post-Easter verses, which are the polar opposites of those pre-Easter verses that speak about the 'rapture of becoming', can provide us with help concerning these questions. Let us take the verse for the second Sunday of Lent first:

> Now speaks unto the human I,
> Mightily revealing
> And setting free its being's force,
> The world-being's rapture of becoming.

If we compare it with its polar opposite verse, that of the third week after Easter, we find:

> Now speaks unto the cosmic All,
> Forgetting self
> And mindful of its origin,
> The growing human I.

Here the strange and mighty polarity is indicated again. That which is outside, namely 'rapture of becoming', turns to the human I, and when the human I begins to unfold after Easter it corresponds to the 'rapture of becoming'. One could almost say that the 'rapture of becoming' is the world I. It speaks to the human I, which, after having been addressed and having gone through the time of Easter, then begins to grow and turns to the cosmic All.

If we go back to verse 47, which provided us with the word *Werdelust*, 'rapture of becoming':

> Now rapture of becoming would arise
> From out the lap of worlds
> Quickening the senses' glory.

we find in the polar opposite verse after Easter:

> From out of narrow selfhood is arisen
> Myself, and finds itself
> As cosmic revelation
> In powers of space and time.

From this it can be seen that the 'rapture of becoming' is the world I, and that in the human being, as though from inside, it corresponds to the human I. Keeping this polarity in mind, let us consider the following:

> From out the lap of worlds would arise (verse 47)
> From out of narrow selfhood is arisen (verse 6)

In these words resurrection begins to resound – the world I strives to arise; the human I is risen. The resurrection has taken place in the course of this period. This is the first point I would like to make.

There is also something else in the verses of Palm Sunday and Easter Sunday, which appears to me to be very important because it is a polarity that concerns all human beings. In one verse it says:

> And beauty gushes from the widths of space (verse 52)

In spite of the fact that images of pain and sorrow arise in our souls during Holy Week, nevertheless 'beauty gushes from the widths of space', and when Easter Sunday comes then what is beauty outside changes into joy from the profound depths of the human soul. Beauty and joy accompany us at Easter time in spite of the Passion. The eternal beauty of existence and the lasting joy of the human heart are both part of the process of resurrection.

Both are part of that great breathing process, of that cosmic laughter and weeping that permeates the whole world-earth-year. The human heart rejoices; it feels jubilant during Easter time and joy breaks forth from human hearts. This is not merely a phrase; it becomes a truth that people begin to experience joy at Easter, just as they do when they look at beauty. This is surely connected with the fact that only a joyful face can be really beautiful and that only beauty can create real joy in the human heart. Well, this much can be said to begin with about this whole world of breath.

Although we live as humans on Earth from conception to death, in actual fact we do not fully permeate our body. We believe we do, and so perhaps it should not be denied at the outset, but in reality we do not live in the substances, or in the anabolic and catabolic processes of composition and decomposition of the body. We live in the earthly and cosmic forces that work through the body, and everything that affects us as mechanical agencies such as the power of gravity or centrifugal forces. At the same time we live within our earthly existence as breath and pulse. By earthly existence I do not mean the physical substances, but existence that is expressed by the body as organisation in the breath and pulse. We live in neither the heart nor the lung, neither the liver nor the kidneys. We carry all these organs in us, and the older we become the more we realise that they are merely ballast that we are quite unable to permeate as yet. As human beings we live in our breathing and our pulse, existing in them both. Therefore, having spoken about breath it is now justifiable to ask where the pulse of the cosmos is to be found.

Turning again to the *Calendar of the Soul*, the first verse, the Easter verse, says:

> When from out of the worlds of space
> The sun doth speak to human sense
> And joy from out of the soul's profundity
> Unites itself with light in the beholding.

Now compare these first four lines with the first three lines of the last verse, that of Palm Sunday:

> When from depths of soul
> The spirit wends to world existence
> And beauty gushes from the widths of space

There is nothing further; but the first verse continues:

> And joy from out of the soul's profundity
> Unites itself with light in the beholding

The statements of spiritual investigation are so exact, for the words 'unites itself with light in the beholding' mean that just as breath and pulse unite with each other, so also the joy that rises out of the soul's depths unites with 'light in the beholding'.

However, the rising, growing light is not identical with the breath of the 'rapture of becoming', the breath of the world I about which we have just spoken, but it is something new. It is the light that illuminates the whole world. It is that light that is spoken of in Genesis when the Word proclaims: 'Let there be light'. At that moment life begins to grow within creation. Life begins to flow, begins to form and shape itself. This is the beginning of all circulation; the beginning of all blood circulation, which leads finally to the heart and the pulse. Consider the cosmic breath outside, the 'rapture of becoming', which unites with the rising earth breath. These two unite in summer, then draw apart again until they are fully separate in the depths of winter. The rising and falling light radiates as pulse through this yearly breathing process of inhaling and exhaling.

The light works in such a way that it creates from within those tides what, since time immemorial, have become the four great festivals of the year: Easter, St John's, Michaelmas and Christmas, or whatever they have been called in pre-Christian and Christian times. In this way we can experience one half of the year exhaling, the other half of the year inhaling. Here (see diagram) is the earthly breath into which work Easter, St John's, Michaelmas and Christmas, and thus the fourfold pulse is born.

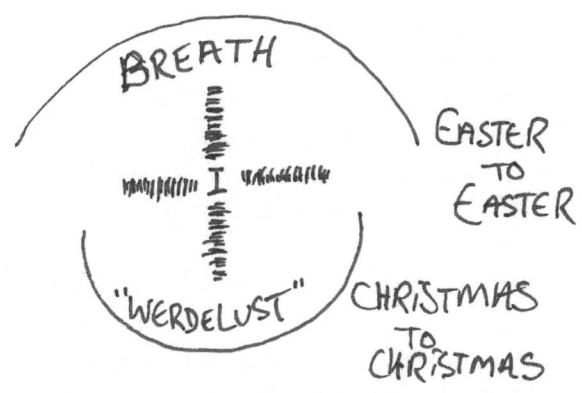

Sketch based on blackboard drawing done at the time.

Here is light, and here is pulse; here is breath, and here 'rapture of becoming', and both meet in the ego. When contemplating this image and observing the interplay of pulse and breath, of world pulse and world breath in which each breath is permeated four times by the pulse, I began to realise that this is the archetypal image of the

Holy Mass that even in the most ancient mysteries has always been celebrated in a fourfold way, in Christian terms as Gospel Reading, Offering, Transubstantiation and Communion. In winter, when the world breath appears after Christmas and the human soul has prepared itself for the Act of Consecration of the year by having gone through the first weeks of January, when the inner strength gained at Christmas begins to radiate outwards, then the eternal gospel is being proclaimed.

Then comes Easter, and what both the human being and the earth receive at Eastertide is carried into the spring, into the Offering. At St John's tide the world breath resounds into this Offering and unites with it in order that in summer the Transubstantiation can take place over the whole Earth and within the human soul. Then follows Michaelmas. The light has now given itself up and begins to fade; the world breath having united itself with the earth breath begins to recede, so that now the human being and Earth receive the Communion. This comes to an end at Christmas, when another new year of the Holy Mass of the earth begins. The gospel reading takes place and everything starts anew.

Thus we can say that at Easter the breathing year of the earth and of the human being begins; and if we want to understand the pulse, then we have to picture the image of the cosmic Mass of the course of the year which starts during the Holy Nights.

These deliberations were a very first beginning in which our approach has been from the realm of nature and the realm of humanity. Next time we shall try to understand it a little more from within. Let us remember the words 'rise, risen, resurrection' for on these everything depends.

Human Breath and
Human Pulse

Lecture given on April 14, 1965

Performances such as those just given can lead deeply into all that should be experienced by human hearts in these days.[1] They call up the images I hinted at on Palm Sunday and make us ready for a conscious experience of Holy Week. In earlier times this experience was different; it was more immediate then, more heartfelt and human. Today it is hardly possible, even among those who understand it, to muster sufficient inner strength, sufficient inner will to lay aside the daily business and turn to what is most fundamental in our existence. We are therefore extremely grateful to our friends for helping to arouse these sentiments and feelings in us.

Before we continue with our reflections about Easter, let me briefly recapitulate what was said on Palm Sunday. You will remember how, with the help of the *Calendar of the Soul*, we tried to approach the world events taking place at this time in the cycle of the year by paying particular attention to the verses for the weeks before and after Easter. We spoke about the double breathing process that takes place within the totality of Earth existence, one rising from the Earth, the other descending from cosmic expanses. And we followed the way these two streams begin to meet each other. It is a decisive fact that these two great breaths set the new year in motion.

Through these verses we then turned our gaze towards everything that confronts us as beauty in the external world and considered the joy of the human heart that streams towards it: beauty from without; joy from within. Beauty and joy accompany these two great breathing processes. Then, discovering something quite remarkable and, I believe, very profound, we realised that behind beauty is that force which in the *Calendar of the Soul* Rudolf Steiner calls *Werdelust*, 'rapture of becoming'; while within or behind joy, the I and the Self arise, corresponding to the 'rapture of becoming'. I briefly added that human beings do not only live in the realm of breath – and nor does the world – but that our breathing is accompanied by the rhythm of the pulse which, at least in most instances, is identical with the rhythm of the heart. If we search consciously for the origin of what we know as the human pulse that is experienced within as the pulse-beat, it is to be found nowhere else save where light weaves in space. The rising and falling of light during the course of the year is mirrored within human beings as the beat of our pulse.

Thus it can be said that just as the breath of the world is revealed by the inhaling and exhaling of the year, so the pulse of the world is experienced as the fourfold beat of the great festivals: St John's, Michaelmas, Christmas and Easter. And this pulse accompanies the breath.

Today we can add that the festivals of the world breath were, and still are, heathen and mighty, while the festivals of the world light are Christian and inward. Just as we must learn to distinguish between world breath and world light outside, and between human breath and human pulse within, so we should learn to differentiate between the heathen elements that still exist in our festivals, and the Christian, inward festivals of light that must gradually replace them. We know that the Christmas festival necessarily contains many heathen traits, as does the festival of Easter. St John's is hardly Christianised as yet, while Michaelmas is only gradually starting to become a Christian, inward festival through the work of Rudolf Steiner. However, concerning the relationship of pulse and breath within the human being and in the world outside, something else should still be added, and it is from this point that I would like to begin today.

In the last lecture it was said that it is not at all true that the human being really lives in their physical body. Before they descended to Earth at birth, the human being is a being of soul and spirit, an individuality, so it would be succumbing to error to believe that they live in material substances such as bone or muscle, or in the organs, or even in such processes as the metabolism or circulation. All the materials, substances and processes are not really our own. We wear them just as we wear a garment that we put on in the morning and take off at night. They are rather like ballast, packing, cover or decoration, and no doubt every person has their own individual substances. In fact, this is a great problem for surgery today. It is especially frustrating for the modern surgeon undertaking organ transplants because they are unable to replace a liver or exchange one kidney for another with the same ease as fitting spare parts to a car. Such people hold the callous view that it is senseless to conceive of the human being as being built individually because they believe that there are no differences in matter. Yet the material substances of our bodies, our organs, tissues and fluids, are only so individual because our ether body is always permeated by our soul-spirit individuality.

Nevertheless, the substances themselves do not belong to us. If we ask where we really live, we have to say that we live in the rhythm of our breathing, although not in the substances of our breathing, and in the rhythm of our pulse. One should make it a point to engage in the meditative task of imagining how one lives as soul in the rhythm of one's breath, how one lives as ego in the rhythm of one's pulse – not in the circulating blood, nor in the substances of the breathing process, but solely in their rhythms.

An important further aspect is that from the very first day, from the moment of our birth, we begin to breathe. We could also say, and it would be quite correct to express it like this, that the moment a child begins to breathe it is born. However this holds good only for the breath, because the pulse begins long before birth at the moment when the fertilised ovum divides into two and begins to grow. We breathe only from the moment of birth, but our pulse begins to beat in the first days of our existence shortly after conception. This is an important difference to notice. Of course, scientists will say that the embryo and the foetus also breathes because the mother's blood provides it with oxygen and removes carbon dioxide, and that therefore this is a breathing process too; but it is, in fact, a process of nutrition. What is called cellular respiration has hardly anything to do with breathing in the sense of inhaling and exhaling air into and out of the depths of the body.

Therefore we can say that the pulse begins soon after conception, whereas breathing begins only at birth, and that we live in both, for they carry us through our existence on Earth. Pulse and breath are the great rhythms within which we truly live. How does the pulse work in us, and we in it? And what does the breath and our soul bring about through the pulse? It is really not very difficult to learn, or rather to experience, how the ego lives and works in the pulse, and how the soul lives and works in the breath. In our pulse and through our blood we find a relationship to the power of uprightness within us that encounters gravity; a relationship that gives rise to the power of will in us. Our pulse binds us to the Earth. It keeps us in the realm of warmth, allowing us to experience will and encounter gravity; it leads downwards into the depths of our existence to where we continually strive to establish our morality. Breath, however, is different. It helps us to find our way into the realm of language, which is aroused in us as children, and through which the power of thinking develops. One path leads from the breath upwards through language to thought and wisdom; the other leads downwards from the pulse through the power of uprightness and gravity, to the will and into morality. Thus from the breath the path leads up to the larynx, where language awakens and speech carries thinking, while from the pulse the path leads in an entirely different direction, in and out, to and from the heart, awakening warmth and entering into that realm which we recognise in life as morality. Let us keep this before us as an image.

Now we must consider a further question: how are breath and pulse related to each other? This can be answered in no other way than by saying that death sets in the moment breathing begins, and that although the pulse continually struggles to counteract the death process, breath is the stronger. Breath destroys; pulse strives to enliven. Breath becomes ever stronger day by day; pulse becomes weaker year by year until finally death occurs when the breath of life has overcome the pulse of existence. So a battle rages continually throughout life; a battle in which the ego endeavours to maintain life by means of the pulse, while the soul tries to destroy life through the breath which increases in power until death overtakes us.

When we reach the point where we are able to grasp this phenomenon consciously, or raise it as an image within us, we are approaching one of the greatest problems that the devout soul has to confront every year, namely the problem of resurrection. St Paul expresses it in the First Letter to the Corinthians by saying:

> But if there be no resurrection of the dead, then is Christ not risen; and if Christ be not risen, then is our preaching vain, and so is your faith.
>
> (1Cor 15:13–14)

Concerning these words, Rudolf Steiner says in the sixth lecture of the cycle *From Jesus to Christ*:

> For what is it that St Paul says? That the whole of Christianity has no justification, and the whole Christian faith no meaning, if the resurrection is not true! That is what is said by Paul, with whom Christianity as a fact of history had its starting-point. And it means that anyone who is willing to give up the resurrection must give up Christianity as Paul understood it.[2]

Taking such an indication seriously means not being content with merely believing in the resurrection of Christ, nor being content with the thought that it cannot be understood anyway, but rather to wrestle actively, especially at Easter, with the question of the meaning of Christ's resurrection. This question is more profound than words can express. It signifies that a God went through death; that he rose and was among his own for forty days. It means that he appeared to them, talked with them and taught them. He appeared not only to individuals, but to two, three, five, even five hundred, and all of them, disciples and apostles, saw him alive. He walked among them, even taking food and allowing Thomas to put his fingers into the wounds. Indeed, this is quite extraordinary.

In the fourth, fifth and sixth lectures of the cycle *From Jesus to Christ*, which Rudolf Steiner held in Karlsruhe in October 1911, he tried with the greatest care and exemplary exactitude to lead his listeners step by step towards the secret of resurrection. He shows, for instance, that the

Christianity of St Paul differs from the Christianity of the disciples and the gospels. This is because the disciples only gradually became aware of the fact, without really grasping its full importance, that the Lord was among them and spoke to them as the Risen One; that he really had risen as the scriptures had prophesied and as he himself had said, but which none of them had believed. Rudolf Steiner shows how at first St Paul did not understand at all what this meant, and how only in the event on the road to Damascus did he suddenly realise: the Lord lives! After that St Paul tried as an initiate to grasp and fully understand what had really happened. He tried to explain it through his own way of thinking by speaking of an old Adam who perishes and a new Adam who resurrects, and how the old Adam must be gradually permeated and replaced by the new Adam.

As a consequence of his spiritual-scientific deductions Rudolf Steiner pointed out the fact that none of the disciples would have been able to think such thoughts, and that St Paul was only able to think in this way because not only was he a believing Jew, he was also a Greek. As a Greek rooted in Greek culture and imbued with the Greek folk spirit, he also experienced sorrow at the loss of the bodily organism. This feeling lived strongly in the Greek people, and they suffered profoundly from the fact that the human body, which they considered the greatest pinnacle of creation by nature and the Godhead, perished at death. In our present context we could say that 'throughout life, breath is stronger than pulse' and therefore the divine form is continually being destroyed. Rudolf Steiner pointed out that everything in our body which is matter, the material and substances of our organs and tissues and so on, is not all-important, because they are only held together during life by that form, that Gestalt, which the Greeks saw perish, and which they valued above all else. Through the event on the road to Damascus, St Paul suddenly realised as an inspiration that the old Adam, the form-body of our physical frame, must be destroyed! The new Adam has arisen and all who give themselves to the new Adam, all who confess to Christ, will be able to experience the renewal of the old Adam through the new Adam. This is the gist of the sermon St Paul gave in Athens. What mattered was to tell the Greek people, the Greek world, that their sorrow had come to an end, for now in the joy of resurrection the old Adam can be replaced by the new Adam. This is the point at issue, but how can we understand it a little better?

May I briefly remind you how in our Christmas lectures we tried to understand the old Adam?[3] In connection with the organ of the human sense of ego, which we described as the human form, we spoke about the spirit-germ, the mighty organism that is prepared for every human being between death and a new birth. We described how both hierarchies and human beings, and the individual human being themselves, work and weave in order to fashion the spirit-germ that every one of us then bears into earthly existence. This form of the spirit-germ becomes the old Adam: it fashions the embryo and its sheaths, building up the foetus so that it gradually takes on human form. With this understanding we can now see that from the day of conception the old Adam is formed and developed in the mother's womb by the human pulse. If we were to describe this fully then world images would appear before us, for in the course of embryonic development, especially during the first days after fertilisation, the most diverse circulations are formed. A yolk-sack circulation appears; a placental circulation is formed; a body-circulation develops and, at the point of intersection of all these circulations on which, so to speak, shines the light of the world, the human form develops as the 'end of God's paths'. Rudolf Steiner once expressed this by saying: 'Thus the gods have the image of the human being before them as their highest ideal, their religion.'⁴ This is what develops in the mother's organism and leads us into the earthly world, giving us the organ of the sense of ego. You will remember that we called this the archetypal phenomenon of all social existence, which opens the possibility of direct and meaningful contact with all human beings.

However, at the very moment we are born and begin to breathe, death sets in. Death gnaws at the old Adam. This moment is heralded by the trumpets of labour, which if we think of a symphony is an exact description. Imagine a symphony by Bruckner or Mahler for instance, where suddenly all the brass and wind instruments strike up, or the sound of the whole orchestra suddenly breaking into a mighty crescendo. This is an image for what happens when the pains of labour set in. At that moment, destruction begins its work and will continue throughout life until the moment of death.

It is through this death process alone, however, that ego-consciousness is created. Ego-consciousness only began to dawn after the Fall, the event that induced breath into the body and forces of destruction into the pulse. Consciousness knocks against the physical organism in breath, through which speech awakens and the power to think is formed, and through the power of thinking the pulse must take hold of gravity and bring about uprightness.

It took many thousands of years until ego-consciousness awakened for the first time in the Greek epoch. However, by the time this happened the old Adam had been destroyed to such an extent, had been so ruined by the power of breath, that the ancient Greek prophecy contained in the myth of Prometheus had come true. This prophecy was that Prometheus would be chained to the rock of the Caucasus and his liver gnawed at every day by an eagle. There could be no better image for what we have tried to describe.

Prometheus was the Titan who stole the fire from heaven, which means he took ego-consciousness from the gods and brought it to men on earth. Therefore he was chained and the eagle, symbolising the breath, gnaws at the source of his blood formation, his liver, and so the process of destruction increases. The story tells how the more the liver was restored during the night, the greater became the power of the eagle's claws, so that there was nothing but death in store for the Titan until Hercules appeared, killing the eagle and setting Prometheus free. Hercules is the symbol of the Sun-power that wanders through the twelve signs of the zodiac; he is an image of the coming Christ. This all leads to an understanding of the old Adam.

When we approach the events in the gospels prior to the Mystery of Golgotha, we find the great heathen epic of Prometheus transformed inwardly into the descriptions of the Christian raisings of the dead. Three great, yet very simple, raisings of the dead are performed by Christ. These are the raising of the youth who is the son of a widow; of the girl who is the daughter of a ruler of the synagogue, and of the man who is the brother of two women: in other words the raising of the youth of Nain, of Jairus' daughter, and of Lazarus, the noble member of the high priests' family.

Although these raisings from the dead are a Christian form of the mighty heathen myth of Prometheus, what do they really portend? We know they are three preliminary steps to the Mystery of Golgotha. Christ indicates that it is not a real death, for when he hears about Lazarus he says: 'Our friend Lazarus sleeps; but I go that I may wake him out of sleep.' He says of Jairus' daughter: 'Weep not; she is not dead but sleeps.' So these are not true raisings from death – from a death that has completely destroyed the human body – but are a public repetition of what had previously only taken place within the mysteries. Therefore, the gospel relates how Christ calls out: 'Lazarus come forth'; how he says to Jairus' daughter: 'Maid, arise', and how he commands the youth of Nain: 'Young man, I say to you, arise.'

What really lies behind this? Christ re-enlivens the breath of these three which had stopped. He re-awakens the process that makes life conscious into the depth of consciousness, and so makes it possible for the process of dying to set in once more after 'death'. What has happened here is what always took place in the mysteries, namely that a death-like sleep befell the neophyte who was to be initiated, and that the hierophant re-awakened the breath by certain spiritual measures that worked down into the physical body. Goethe expressed this same process later when he wrote:

> As long as you do not attain
> This dying and becoming,
> You are but a dull guest
> On the dark earth.

The decisive point for all three – the youth of Nain, Jairus' daughter, and Lazarus – was the process of 'dying and becoming'. Only in the Mystery of Golgotha, which followed as a fourth event after the three preparatory ones, is there a re-awakening not only of the breath, but also of the pulse. Now we know what is meant when it is said that the spirit germ, the old Adam, cannot be reawakened. He has become the cross, but on this cross the roses have begun to bloom. The resurrection begins and death becomes life. Easter jubilation – which passed unheard by human beings, but was heard by all the gods – resounded through the cosmos: Christ rose; the new Adam was born; the first Easter began.

This is as far as I would like to go today. We shall continue our attempts to understand the new Adam, and, with the help of Rudolf Steiner's insight, I hope it will be possible to achieve this to some degree.

Easter, the Festival of Resurrection

Lecture given on Easter Sunday, April 18, 1965

Now Easter has finally come. This year we have tried to approach it in a special way by attempting to take the first steps towards understanding that great secret that lies hidden in the simple word 'resurrection'. Time and again the human spirit tries, although often in vain, to reach an understanding of the riddle of resurrection. But whatever contribution we try to make to advance our understanding, whether as the fruit of thinking or as a meditative effort using the sources opened for us by Rudolf Steiner, will only be a stepping stone towards the glory of resurrection that lies ahead of humanity, perhaps only at the end of Earth evolution. Therefore we should remember that it can only ever be with hesitant, imperfect or incomplete, yet nonetheless striving steps that we endeavour to approach this secret. However, the Easter impulse, the tender dawn of the Easter jubilation, will always give us the courage to go forward, resolutely treading the path in pursuit of this mystery.

A week ago, on Palm Sunday, we approached it from a specific angle through Rudolf Steiner's *Calendar of the Soul*, trying to grasp what we called the world breath and world pulse from the point of view of the cosmos and of nature. Then, on Holy Wednesday, we proceeded a step further in trying to understand the breath and pulse in human beings, and we were helped in this endeavour by the mythological image of Prometheus chained to the rock, haunted day after day by the eagle, a symbol for the breath, eating into his liver and thus into his life. As an image this is an accurate analogy for what happens in the human being, for during life the breath also gnaws constantly at the power of the pulse, eating into the power of the blood. It was even expressed by saying that a person's life between birth and death is in reality an unceasing battle between the gnawing breath and the continuously renewed blood, and that the breath gains the upper hand and so leads to death.

Death is the inevitable end for Prometheus as a result of the eagle gnawing at his liver, as it is for everyone by the breath eating into their pulse. At death the form of the human body disintegrates, and we realised that this human form is identical with that sensory-supersensible formation that we had described earlier at Christmas, and which we called to mind again in the last lecture. It is what Rudolf Steiner called the spirit-germ, which is created anew for every person during the time between death and a new birth. It is the spirit-germ into which is woven all human destiny, the work of the hierarchies and all those who were connected with us during our former life, thus bringing about a mighty spirit form that becomes smaller and smaller until the moment it unites with the physical germ of the developing human being that is forming in the mother's womb.

We described how the spirit-germ is received by the pulse, the circulation of the blood, as a spiritual form, and also how breath sets in at the moment of birth and, with it, the process of death that accompanies us throughout our lives. If, as a first outline, we try to visualise the spirit-germ pictorially, we must imagine it as the human form.

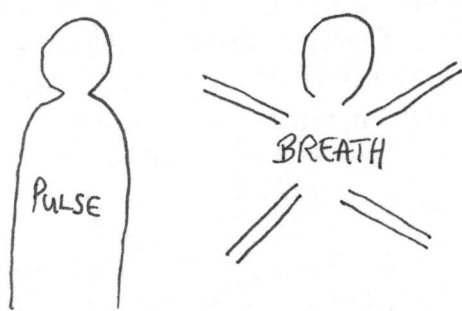

Sketch based on blackboard drawing done at the time.

Of course, it is extremely primitive to draw it like this, nevertheless it is the human form consisting of head and body. Now the moment breath sets in, which can be observed and studied by comparative anatomy, the human form extends into the shape of the limbs, and so it is justified to write 'pulse' here and to call this 'breath'. Here we can see immediately that the formation of the limbs represents the formation of the Earth, for it is only by means of our limbs, especially our legs, but also our arms, that we become citizens of the Earth. This form is still the image of the human being as it is born in the image of God. However, from the hour of birth the breath begins to gnaw at this form so that in the course of the first years of life the 144 (12 x 12) pulse beats per minute that the child has before birth are reduced by half, and thereafter we have to be content with 72 beats. This has to be considered in a first attempt to grope towards the secret of resurrection.

This differentiation between pulse and breath, between the cosmic light and cosmic breath which permeate the world, is essential, for without it we cannot approach what St Paul called the old and the new Adam and, two thousand years later, Rudolf Steiner called the 'phantom'. We should know that the phantom described by Rudolf Steiner is identical with what St Paul called the old and the new Adam. Rudolf Steiner spoke extensively about the nature of the phantom in the lecture cycle *From Jesus to Christ*, and we will now try to wrestle for an understanding of what is meant by the phantom. In the sixth lecture Rudolf Steiner says:

> But the more clairvoyance is developed in our time, the clearer will it be that the physical forces and substances laid aside are not the whole physical body, for its complete configuration could never derive from them alone. To these substances and forces there belongs something else, best called the 'phantom' of the human being. This phantom is the form-shape which as a spiritual texture works up the physical substances and forces so that they fill out the form which we encounter as the human being on the physical plane.[1]

What is described here as the phantom is called the spirit-germ in Rudolf Steiner's later writings.

It is important to recognise at the outset that the phantom is the same as the old Adam; that figure which was given to humanity as a physical form by the gods. In the course of those lectures, Rudolf Steiner even said that we were not in fact meant to fill this form with earthly, material substance, but that it should have remained a sensory-supersensible form, which means a physical and yet invisible one. It was only as a result of the Fall that this form no longer remained physical but became material: originally it was only physical. The Divine Thought did not intend human beings to possess the physical-material bodies we do today. However, while the Fall brought about a densification of soul-spiritual substance, a deeper immersion of the human ego-being into the minerals and substances of the earth, it also awakened something which everyone experiences today as their ego-consciousness. It is of great importance to try once again to grasp what it is that makes us conscious. The materialisation of the form of the body, of the phantom, brought about our self-consciousness, our ego-consciousness, for in coming up against this corporeality, which was becoming ever denser, in knocking against it, the ego awoke to a consciousness of itself, to its own self-consciousness. Rudolf Steiner spoke about this in the seventh lecture of *From Jesus to Christ* in the following way:

> We cannot comprehend Christianity unless we understand that at the time when the events in Palestine took place, humanity on Earth had reached a stage where the decadence of the physical body was at its peak, and where, because of this, the whole evolution of humanity was threatened with the danger that the ego-consciousness – the specific achievement of the Earth evolution – would be lost. If this process had continued unchanged, the destructive element would have penetrated ever more deeply into the human bodily organism, and people born after the time when the events of Palestine were due would have had to live with an ever-duller feeling of the ego.[2]

We can now see that human beings were created in a form that corresponded to the rhythm of our pulse, the cosmic rhythm of 12 x 12. This form was meant to be a true microcosm, both human and divine. However, it went through the Fall and humanity became mature for the Earth. The human breath began its gnawing work, creating powers of destruction that made consciousness possible until, within this general consciousness, self-consciousness appeared. Yet parallel with humanity's rising self-consciousness came those destroying powers that, working ever more strongly, caused ever greater disintegration of the first God-created human form, which resulted in the gradual dimming of ego-consciousness. The repercussion of this awakening thinking was the progressive destruction of the God-willed form that still held the human being together.

I am aware that some found difficulty in understanding why it is that pulse and blood are linked with gravity, and breath with speech and thought. It is not possible to enlarge on this fully now, other than to touch on the subject by repeating that light and sound, the two primeval powers that permeate all creation, should be understood as being active in pulse and breath. It is the light in the pulse that encounters gravity and thereby creates the power of uprightness, and it is the sound in the breath that encounters disintegration in the chemical structure. Thus the human form, which Rudolf Steiner here calls the phantom, proceeds step by step towards gravity and disintegration. I have described all this from a number of angles because I believe that these are fundamental steps to be taken in order gradually to reach the veiled image behind which the riddle of resurrection is hidden.

You see, what is said by Rudolf Steiner in the passage we have just read – namely that the phantom had decayed so far by the time of Christ's incarnation that had Christ *not* incarnated then humanity's experience of the ego would have grown dimmer and perhaps been lost altogether – is also described in the four gospels. In the last lecture we referred to the three raisings from the dead: the raising of Jairus' daughter, of the youth of Nain, and of Lazarus, the brother of Mary and Martha.

What Rudolf Steiner tried to express in the passage just quoted is revealed in these three events. We are concerned here with three persons: a girl who has just attained the age of twelve, a youth who is about sixteen or seventeen years old, and a mature man, all of whom die without apparent reason, without illness. It seems that these three are persons whose forces of life have begun to dwindle away.

Concerning these healings of the sick, the gospels do not say what kind of illness, sin or error is involved, but simply describe what happened: the maiden dwindled away, the youth died, and about Lazarus of Bethany nothing is said except that after his death and burial his sisters sent messengers to Christ saying: 'Our brother has died, come and help.' If we try to read the gospels very carefully we can find signs which perhaps allow us to discover what the issue really is. The raising of Jairus' daughter is told in the three so-called synoptic gospels, and each time it is preceded quite pointedly by the story of the woman who suffered from an issue of blood for twelve years. In a rather modern way it is even noted that she spent all her money on doctors, but none could help her. Yet it is emphasised that she had suffered the illness for twelve years, which means that she had suffered the issue of blood for as many years as the daughter of Jairus had been alive. In this way both events are linked in the composition of the three gospels, and we may ask what this means. We are told that when Christ is called by Jairus and he sets off to go to the daughter, the woman touches the hem of his garment and he realises that at that moment a power has gone out of him. At that same moment the woman's issue of blood ceases and she is healed. Now it is pertinent to ask what the matter with this woman had been. The simple answer is that she suffered from a continuous menstruation that would not stop. If we ask when does the monthly period normally cease in the life of any woman, one answer is: when pregnancy begins.

However, a woman becomes pregnant only when a new spirit-germ, the phantom of an incarnating child, descends and takes up its dwelling in the mother's organism. At that moment the monthly period stops. This is what happened here, because when the woman touched the border of Christ's garment the powers of the phantom streamed into her and stemmed the flow of blood. We can therefore say that having reached the age of twelve, the daughter of Jairus should have started her monthly menstrual flow, but was dying because her phantom did not have the strength to hold the blood. Consequently the blood is overcome by gravity; it flows down and with it the girl's powers of life ebb away just as the powers of life of the woman flowed away. Christ touches the girl and she is healed.

The case of the youth of Nain is similar, and yet different. Rudolf Steiner once said that the youth of Nain whom Christ raised was the youth of Sais, who in a former life had been unable to recognise the Being of Man in the mysteries. He had been rejected in the Egyptian mysteries and was now reborn as the son of a widow. The absence of a father signifies that the power to cast one's anchor into the earth is missing: the will is lacking. In a similar way to the daughter of Jairus, in whom the blood is overcome by gravity, so in the youth of Nain the blood is overcome, but in his case by levity, and it becomes volatile. Therefore Christ Jesus had to come in order to touch the youth and heal his phantom, his physical body, so that he can be restored to the widow, his mother.

The secret of Lazarus' death is different yet similar. What lies hidden in this secret is later given as an image when, after entering Jerusalem, Christ curses the fig tree that bears no fruit and the next morning the tree is seen to have withered and died. For when Lazarus the rich youth approached Christ and asked 'Master, what shall I do?', Christ replied 'Give away all your treasures', which meant that he should give away all the treasures of wisdom that he had gained by being one of the elders of the Jews. He is asked to become like a fig tree without fruit. For a man whose phantom body is disintegrating it is impossible to do this, but Lazarus does it nevertheless. It is an immense sacrifice for him to relinquish this wisdom in the name, one could say, of all who still drew upon the old wisdom, because in doing so he withers away. He dies. The blood, the pulse, cannot hold its own against the onslaught of the new that opens up on letting go of the old.

Each of these three is raised from death. These raisings, however, are nothing else than the renewal of that figure which will hold the blood together in order that it can meet, at least for a while, the onslaught of the gnawing waves of breath. We can also say that these three are reawakened by the abounding power of Christ's love. This is indicated in the gospels when Christ tells Jairus: 'Fear not, believe only.' When Christ sees the widow, the gospel says: 'And when the Lord saw her, he had compassion on her, and said unto her: "Weep not."'; and when he comes to Lazarus' sister, it says: 'When Jesus therefore saw her weeping and the Jews also weeping that came with her, he groaned in the spirit, and was troubled.' The all-pervading love of Christ springs forth in eyes, hands and heart, and from it flows the strength for the renewal of the phantom of these three.

The point at issue here is not that these three alone should have been raised, but that what happened to them should also happen for all people. Rudolf Steiner once spoke in a remarkable way about these three raisings from the dead, indicating that we should see in them how the three great post-Atlantean cultures were healed.[3] Christ takes up what had decayed in the Indian culture and heals it by raising Jairus' daughter. Similarly, the decaying Egyptian-Babylonian culture is healed by reviving the youth of Nain. What this means is that these were the representatives of humanity's past in whom the phantom was re-illumined. But what should happen to humanity of the fourth and fifth epochs, for it was also necessary to work into the future? This was the great question that presented itself at that time, cosmically, so to speak, and which was to be solved by the Christ-event on Golgotha.

In order to understand this more fully we shall have to approach these immense problems from yet another side. You will remember that at Christmas we considered the two Jesus children, and how from a new aspect we tried to understand what the Nathan and the Solomon beings were and are. Of the Nathan-Jesus child, who was born at the turning point of time and was welcomed by the shepherds, we know that he received an earthly body for the first time. This was that ego-being that had been preserved since the first beginnings of humanity; since the time of Adam and Eve during the Lemurian age. He did not go through the Fall with the rest of humanity but waited untouched until he descended to Earth at the turning point of time. This being then became the bearer of the ego of the Solomon-Jesus child in his twelfth year. Only in his thirtieth year, as Jesus of Nazareth, did he become the vehicle for the Christ-spirit at the baptism in the river Jordan.

Let us now place this very earnestly before our spiritual eyes. Here is an untouched being that descends to Earth for the first time and permeates itself with earthly substance, but brings with it an untouched, blameless, innocent ego, into whose sheaths the Christ enters. Concerning this Rudolf Steiner says in the seventh lecture of *From Jesus to Christ*:

> It came to pass that one man, who was the bearer of the Christ, had gone through such a death that after three days the specifically mortal part of the physical body had to disappear, and out of the grave there rose the body which is the force-bearer of the physical, material parts. The body that was really intended for man by the rulers of Saturn, Sun and Moon – the pure phantom of the physical body

with all the attributes of the physical body – this it was that
rose out of the grave. So was given the possibility of that
spiritual genealogy of which we have spoken.

Let us think of the body of Christ that rose out of
the grave. Just as from the body of Adam the bodies of
earthly humanity are descended, in so far as these have
the body that crumbles away, even so are the spiritual
bodies, the phantoms for all people, descended from that
which rose out of the grave. And it is possible to establish
a relationship with Christ through which the earthly
human being can bring into their otherwise decaying
physical body this phantom which rose out of the grave
of Golgotha. It is possible for the human being to receive
into their organism those forces which then rose from
the grave, just as through his physical organism at the
beginning of the Earth evolution, as a consequence of the
Luciferic forces, they received the organism of Adam.

It is this that Paul wishes to say. Just as we, through
our place in the stream of physical evolution, inherit the
physical body in which the destruction of the phantom,
the force-bearer, is gradually taking place, so from the
pure phantom that rose out of the grave we can inherit
what we have lost. We can inherit it, can clothe ourselves
with it, as we clothed ourselves with the first Adam; we
can become one with it. Thereby we can go through a
development by means of which we can climb upwards
again, even as before the Mystery of Golgotha we had
descended in evolution. In other words, that which was
taken from us through the Luciferic influence can be
given back to us through its presence as the risen body of
Christ.[4]

Here we are coming a little closer to what we are trying
to understand. Out of the grave arose the new Adam, the
phantom, renewed through Christ indwelling the body of

Jesus of Nazareth. Can we understand this even further? To do so we will have to add yet another aspect. This year, as a preparation towards Easter, we read the Gospel of St Mark, which I believe was very important, and yesterday evening during the Bible evening and again this morning we heard the passage which that relates how the three women go to the grave early on the morning of Easter Sunday. Finding that the stone has been rolled away they look into the sepulchre but cannot find the body of Christ. Instead they see a young man sitting at the right side of the grave.

The question now arises: who is this youth? Here Rudolf Steiner gives a very clear answer. In the lectures on the Gospel of St Mark he refers to a previous chapter of the gospel that mentions this youth in the description of Maundy Thursday night and the arrest of Christ by his persecutors. He quotes the passage:

> And there followed him closely a certain young man, who wore a fine linen garment over his bare body, and they seized him. But he let go of the linen garment and fled naked. (Mk 14:51–52)

and then he continues:

> Who is this young man? Who was it who escaped? Who is it who appears here, next to Christ Jesus, nearly unclothed, and then slips away unclothed? This is the youthful cosmic impulse, it is the Christ who slips away, who now has only a loose connection with the Son of Man. Much is contained in the fifty-first and fifty-second verses. The new impulse retains nothing of what former times were able to wrap around man. It is the entirely naked, new cosmic impulse of earth evolution. It remains near Jesus of Nazareth, and we find it again at the beginning of the sixteenth chapter ... 'And as they entered

the tomb they saw a young man sitting on the right side, clothed in a long white garment; and they were startled' (Mk 16:5). This is the same youth. In the whole artistic composition of the gospels nowhere else does this youth confront us, the youth who slips away at the moment when they condemn the Son of Man, who is there again when the three days are over, and who from now onwards is active as the cosmic principle of the earth.[5]

Summarising all this we can say that the spirit-being of Christ partly leaves the sheath of Jesus of Nazareth at the moment men lay hands on Him, and what is left is the sheath of the Nathan being of Jesus of Nazareth, forsaken by the cosmic impulse. So it is the Son of Man who goes through death. He is accompanied by the Son of God, but it is the Son of Man who is crucified, suffers death and is placed in the grave. What happened is described by Rudolf Steiner in the eighth lecture of *From Jesus to Christ*:

> When the body was taken down from the Cross, the parts were still coherent, but they had no connection with the phantom; the phantom was completely free of them. When the body became permeated with certain substances, which in this case worked quite differently from the way in which they affect any other body that is embalmed, it came to pass that after the burial the material parts quickly volatilised and passed over into the elements. Hence the disciples who looked into the grave found the linen clothes in which the body had been wrapped, but the phantom, on which the evolution of the ego depends, had risen from the grave.[6]

So you see, the resurrection – and I beg you to take these words in full earnestness – the resurrection is the salvation and renewal of the phantom. However, the Risen

One himself is connected with the Christ impulse. These belong together just as breath and pulse belong together in the human being, and yet they are twofold. The phantom is saved through the fact that the untouched being of Jesus of Nazareth, who as the Nathan-Jesus child was born for the first time in human form at the turning point of time, is permeated during the three years by the power, strength and light of the Christ-spirit. Christ has risen and is the Risen One: the phantom is saved and is the resurrection.

We must gradually come to realise this if we wish to approach these questions with a certain degree of clarity.

You see, the Mystery of Golgotha was really a further step continuing on from three preliminary steps that we already know.[7] Once during the Lemurian age and twice during the later Atlantean age – at its beginning and again at its end – powers of love streamed down to humanity as healing for all humanity through the Nathan being that had received the Christ-spirit like a cup.

In the first act of healing, during Lemuria, the senses were soothed; in the second act of healing, the organs were harmonised, and in the third act of healing, thinking, feeling and willing within the human soul were brought into order. Then a further step followed when this being took on an earthly body and sacrificed itself once more in being permeated by the Christ-spirit. And thereby the human form, the spirit-germ, was renewed. It is in this light that we can speak of a new Adam in the sense intended by St Paul, or about a new phantom body as Rudolf Steiner meant it to be understood. The secret of the phantom is the secret of the fourth deed of sacrifice of the Nathan being, for it is the Son of Man who goes through death and through whom the resurrection, the renewal of the human form created in the image of God, now takes place. We can now understand that at the time the moon left the earth, when male and female were created and the breath came into being and began to gnaw at man's pulse, already then that ego that remained pure was retained. It accompanied all humanity and through the fact that Christ ensouled himself in it, it became the threefold healer until it descended to earth for the fourth deed of healing.

At that moment something happened which, following on from the end of the last lecture, we can contemplate as the Cross permeated by death on which the roses have begun to bloom through the resurrection. You see, it is the purpose of true Rosicrucianism to endeavour to give those who have dedicated themselves to it the foundations whereby they can connect themselves to the new Adam, for the new Adam is neither gained by blood nor kinship, nor can it be acquired by any earthly force. The new Adam works wherever the human spirit begins to triumph over need and hardship; over gravity and levity; over every earthly power. The new Adam has a part in everyone who sets out to become a true human being in the sense of the Rose Cross. What happened at the turning point of time takes place today in every person of goodwill, for Christ walks today through the Earth-sphere as the Risen One. He is here; he is risen. We humans, however, have the task of taking up what is revealed in the resurrection and becoming what in truth we already are: brothers and sisters of Christ.

Tomorrow we shall try to round all this off, drawing further conclusions from a few more aspects of these facts, thoughts and ideas with which we began a week ago.

Earthly Creation, Human Form and Human Ego

Lecture given on April 19, 1965

Tonight we will conclude our present efforts to understand the great mystery described by the word 'resurrection'. What we undertook this Easter was rather exceptional and at times very complicated, even confusing, especially when occasionally it contradicted our ordinary way of thinking. This was because we were attempting to relate sense-perceptible phenomena to supersensible events so as to bring out the importance of what lies behind the riddle of resurrection. Easter demands this of us because in this festival we are confronted with supersensible events taking place in the realm of the senses. As an example of this we need only read in the Gospel of St Luke how two disciples on their way to Emmaus are suddenly joined by a third, an unknown man who talks with them and explains the events that have so shaken them. The man accompanies them into the house, sits down at the table and breaks bread with them, and then he disappears. Or how on the same day the Risen One appears to the disciples in the Upper Room, and not only do they see and recognise him but they also give him a piece of fish and some honey, which he eats, and then he disappears again. This is Easter; the supersensible is so anchored in the sensory that it can be perceived.

In an Easter lecture Rudolf Steiner once said the following:

> During the fifth post-Atlantean epoch a new tendency has been at work, a tendency towards a scientific knowledge that is adapted to the power of human reason and judgement; and now it is time that this should go further and develop into a knowledge of the supersensible world. For the event of Golgotha is one that falls absolutely within the supersensible world. And the event of Damascus, as Paul experienced it, is an event that can be understood only out of supersensible ideas. Whether one can truly feel something of the Christ Impulse, or not, depends on an understanding of these events. In our present age, each individual ought to examine themselves and ask whether, at the time we call 'Easter', they are able to find a connection to supersensible knowledge. For Easter should remind us, by the very way its date is determined, to look up from the earthly to what is beyond the Earth. People of modern times have confined their view of what is beyond the Earth to concepts derived from mathematics, mechanics, and more recently spectral analysis. These sciences are the groundwork upon which they try to build up knowledge of all that is beyond the Earth. They no longer feel themselves united with those worlds, nor have they any idea that the Christ descended from them when he entered into the person of Jesus.[1]

In the lectures last week we tried to follow this Pauline attitude because it seems to be an essential element in our endeavours. It is an attitude in which a new attempt is made to represent the existence of supersensible phenomena in the realm of the senses. Therefore I began by considering cosmic pulse and breath and trying to understand human pulse and breath. We also tried to reach beyond the perception of purely sensory phenomena to an understanding of the phantom, that physical yet supersensible form that holds together the material and substance of our mineral body so that it becomes visible, and because of which we can speak of a physical-material corporeality. Now, if we wish to understand a further aspect of the phantom, which despite being the physical form is invisible to human eyes, is it beyond the bounds of possibility to develop imaginative thought in order to do so? Perhaps the following approach may prove helpful.

The alchemists (by which I do not mean the charlatans but the genuine alchemists) spoke truthfully about the philosopher's stone some four, five or six hundred years ago. They themselves did not search for a stone (only the charlatans did that) for the true alchemists knew very well what the philosopher's stone really was. If they had been asked, as was customary among initiated alchemists, they would have said that it is nothing other than that element that everyone carries in themself, which permeates everything living, everything organic. The philosopher's stone is simply carbon, one of the most essential building stones of all organic and inorganic substances. If one were to have asked an alchemist about the form of the human body, the structure of the old and new Adam (which he would have well understood), he would have said: 'Observe carbon and understand that diamond, graphite and black coal are one and the same. Know, however, that to really understand the nature of diamond you have to imagine it still more transparent than it appears, for in truth it consists of nothing other than geometrically formed light. If you can imagine and grasp this, then you will realise that a crystal is an archetypal image of salt, and that it is a form of light. Then you will also see how during the course of the earth's development this light form darkened, becoming tangible, visible graphite, and later changing to become coal.'

In the path from diamond via graphite to coal, we can see the transformation from what the alchemist calls salt into what he calls ash. Diamond is still the purest, almost intangible, almost invisible salt, because it is formed out of pure light. Yet the denser carbon becomes, the more substance is deposited in it, the more it becomes ash. In the same way the old Adam evolved out of what was once the pure Adam, the untouched human form, and it breaks up because ash components are mixed into its form. Rudolf Steiner expressed this in the eighth lecture of *From Jesus to Christ*:

> We said yesterday that the human phantom, the primal form which takes up into itself the material elements that fill out the physical body and are laid aside at death, had degenerated in the course of time up to the Mystery of Golgotha. In a certain way, we may grasp the idea of this degeneration as follows: At the beginning of human evolution it was intended that the phantom should remain untouched by the material elements that the human being takes up as nutrition from the animal, plant and mineral kingdoms. But it did not remain untouched. For the Luciferic influence brought about a close connection between the phantom and the forces that the human being takes in through earthly development; a connection particularly with the ashy constituents. The result was that the phantom, while continuing to accompany humanity in its further evolution, was strongly drawn to these ashy constituents, and instead of adhering to the etheric body, it attached itself to these products of disintegration.[2]

We will now take a further step and try to understand the phantom that had become a centre of attraction for the particles of ash. We have learned that the breath gnaws continuously at the phantom, just as the eagle gnaws at Prometheus' liver. Through this continual erosion of the pulse that carries the phantom, the phantom was doomed to perish at the time of the Mystery of Golgotha. In an entirely different context Rudolf Steiner spoke about the seven life-processes. He described how in the course of earth evolution, through Ahrimanic and Luciferic influences, these seven life-processes became something different from what the gods had intended. In describing the first three processes of breathing, warming and nourishing he said that breathing became consumption, warming became burning, and nourishing became depositing. Then he went on to say:

> We do not breathe as we would breathe if only regular, progressive, divine-spiritual impulses were active in the breath – the impulses mentioned at the beginning of the Old Testament; more than the power of Yahweh is active in our breathing. For, during the Atlantean period, ahrimanic forces caused our breathing system to be modified and these modifications now affect the way we breathe. Thus, we not only breathe, we consume our organism. And we experience this consumption as a kind of feeling of well-being. It is a fact that, during the course of our life between birth and death, we use our breathing process more energetically than was intended. The consumption of our life forces is very closely connected to this ahrimanic influence. One can say, broadly speaking, that if it were not for this ahrimanic influence we would not inhale as much oxygen in a given period of time, and the consumption of our organism associated with the process of ageing would not be as intense as it now is – I mean ageing in the sense that it involves something that can be seen and not just the passage

of years. This is related in many ways to ahrimanic influences on the process of breathing.

Because of ahrimanic influences in our organism, things are burnt up more quickly than a regular evolution would dictate: consumption is a kind of incineration. We actually burn ourselves up. Through ahrimanic influence, nourishment includes the forming of deposits, so that our nourishment is not merely processed, but is also stored away in our organism as virtually foreign matter.[3]

What the breathing process does within human beings is clearly described here: it consumes. This means that our powers of life are continually being consumed by the breathing process. Warming changes from warmth into fire and, as Rudolf Steiner expresses it, human beings 'consumes' themselves. As a further consequence of this consuming and burning, nourishing becomes depositing. You see, if we consider this and gradually learn to comprehend it, then we will realise that what was once the 'diamond' of the phantom had to change into 'graphite' and become black coal through consuming, burning and depositing.

Taking this new aspect we are now able to grasp what we tried to understand yesterday concerning the blood, namely the three raisings from the dead described in the New Testament: that of Jairus' daughter, of the youth of Nain, and Lazarus of Bethany. I have already pointed out that these three passed away without illness, without apparent cause, and that by their deaths they were each representative of earlier epochs of humanity's history in which the phantom had disintegrated. Through laying his hand on them and calling them back from death, Christ caused the power of the renewed phantom in him to be transferred to these three, and in them arose a first inkling of what St Paul called the new Adam.

From what has just been said about consuming, burning and depositing we can take a further step, a physiological one, to discover what really happened in these three cases. In Jairus' daughter it was as if the power of the blood dwindled away when she entered puberty. The power of the blood was extinguished because the breath was so strong that it had consumed the body after only twelve years. When considering the youth of Nain we said that he had been a widow's son and so lacked a father; he did not have the will for earth existence and consequently was burned up after sixteen or seventeen years, dying as a result. For Lazarus, who had sacrificed all the treasures of wisdom he had gathered, life could not continue because everything that had become deposit in him carried him into the grave. We could say that all the healings and raisings from the dead in the New Testament are in fact endeavours by Christ to give new life to the seven life-processes in their archetypal form. These things offer potential for a new recognition that we shall have to acquire in order to understand the realities, right down to physical details.

This has brought us closer to an understanding of human pulse and human breath. Let us now recollect the first lecture in which, with the help of the *Calendar of the Soul*, we tried to understand the processes of cosmic breathing and cosmic pulse. You may remember that we asked ourselves many questions. What, for example, is meant by *Werdelust*, the 'rapture of becoming', in the two verses immediately prior to Passiontide? And what is it in the cosmos that comes to meet the exhaled breath of the earth? What is the light of the sun that ascends and descends four times in the course of the year, permeating the great inhaling and exhaling breath of the year with light? What is this 'cosmic breath', and whence did it originate? Is it still in the same state as on the first day of creation, or has it perhaps become something quite new and different, perhaps even akin to another cloak or sheath of the earth? Rudolf Steiner spoke about this on many occasions, but in one lecture he said:

> When the Earth was emerging, rising, as it were, from the darkness of cosmic space as a glowing heat, the earliest human forms in this space of glowing heat were heat entities in themselves. Looking back with a clairvoyant eye on human beings as they then existed, you would first of all find this early beginning of humanity as if the whole heat sphere had many, many currents in it.[4]

This is a description of the Earth before the preceding stages of Old Moon, Old Sun and Old Saturn. Earth was then a mighty body of warmth that reached the present orbit of Saturn, and it was nothing but humanity itself – humanity formed out of warmth, the human form fashioned from currents of warmth, which looked approximately like this:

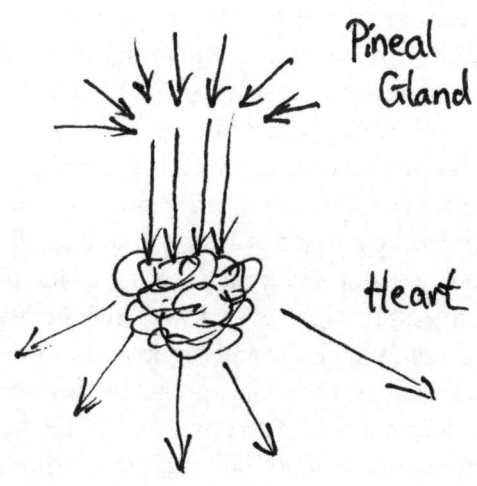

Sketch based on blackboard drawing done at the time.

Currents of warmth streamed in from the periphery to a certain point from which they then flowed down, forming a vortex of warmth, and radiated outwards. Here we see a process that is also found in the development of the human embryo. Rudolf Steiner tells us that here is the archetypal organ of what later became the pineal gland, while below it is the archetypal form of what later became the heart. The earth evolved from millions and millions of such human forms. It is the archetypal form. It is the seed of the phantom that was formed here and which later developed between the heart and the great warmth organ, the pineal gland. Warmth became denser, and from it came both air and radiating light. Then air condensed and gave rise to water, and just as light came from air, so sound or tone evolved from the watery element. Thus step by step the entire organism of the earth evolved through a process of condensing and separating. Animals, plants, minerals and mountains all evolved in this way until finally – although always present from the beginning – the human being appeared. Everything that condensed too early became plant, mineral and animal.

In the Ephesian mysteries, where above all else Earth evolution was taught as a manifestation of the power of the Word, pupils were given an image of this development. They were taught that during the early Lemurian period the Earth was not yet solid. What had begun to condense was still surrounded by a vast fluid atmosphere of albuminous vapour, which was not yet liquid but gaseous and permeated with a little moisture. However, it was living matter, living organic albumen, which extended outwards a long way; so far, in fact, that it reached the moon. In this albuminous atmosphere something lit up from time to time that became green and then disappeared, became green again and then vanished once more. It was the first coming and going of spring and autumn.

Within this process of greening, plants sprouted and withered away again. These were not plants that grew on the earth but floated in a gleaming, fluorescent sphere. Into this plant realm worked what today is the silica process, and in this atmosphere were also denser parts that could be seen as ascending and descending clouds. These clouds contained lime which condensed, formed animal shapes, and then dissolved again. In this floating sphere of albumen many shapes were formed so that fluorescent plant life and solidifying animal life developed. Processes of breathing and nutrition were still one and the same at that time, because animal, plant and human beings inhaled and exhaled albumen. But step by step, as the process of condensation unfolded, forms became permanent, plants took root, animals were born and died, until gradually everything took on organic form.

Nothing now remains of this creative power, except rhythm. What we call cosmic pulse today is just a remnant of what was once cosmic plant existence, and what we call cosmic breath is what remains of those traces of creation that are closely associated with the substances of lime and silica, out of which the limestone, granite and sandstone mountains arose, as well as all the animals of the earth. Plants became organs of the earth's surface. And amidst all this is the human being.

What happened to the cosmic breathing process that had run down? When the cosmic breath approaches the earth in spring, it calls the beings that had formerly lived in it to awaken: plants begin to sprout and animals are born. A memory is evoked and revitalised by the cosmic breath so that the elemental beings, the sylphs, undines and salamanders, emerge out of the earth. These exhale so as to meet what had once been their mother sheath. With their help plants become green, animals awaken, and light rises and fades away. Thus development continues because the memory of creation can still be called up and enlivened.

Just as we can look back to our youth, so in spring the Earth remembers its former creative power and strength, but as a memory picture. A remnant of this is the mysterious interplay of breathing, continually weaving between plants and animals by virtue of the fact that animals exhale carbon dioxide and plants take it in and transform it through light to provide oxygen. Animals and humans then inhale the oxygen, transforming it into carbon dioxide again. So all organic existence can still be maintained by this giving and taking: through the decaying that emanates from animals, and the enlivening that reappears in plants. This is further mirrored in the human being in what we called the 'breath that gnaws at the pulse of our existence', for while the gnawing breath induces decay, the radiating blood enlivens. Just as everything that flowers outside in nature is connected with chlorophyll, so everything that is enlivened within us is connected with almost the same substance: red haemoglobin.

Just as creation slowly evolved externally, so ash – which we have now come to see as an image of carbon – gradually developed within the human being. Now we face a great question: why is it that ash develops in the human being through the fact that breathing changes into consuming, warming into burning and nourishing into depositing? Rudolf Steiner gave an important indication as to this in the lecture from which we quoted earlier:

> What made the ash principle, the mineral element, flow into this substance? It was the thought which makes sound, tone, into word which pushed ash into the human bodies. In Atlantean times, when vapour and mist surrounded everything, the things human beings said were not the one and only articulated language for they

were able to understand the language of soughing trees, trickling wells ... The meaning, the significance of words pushed the ash resulting in the combustion process into this living matter, and as the skeletal system grew more and more dense towards the end of the Atlantean age human beings were more and more filled with thoughts, with self-awareness. Intellectualism lit up, and they came to be more and more self-aware.[5]

We may understand this indication better if we realise that thoughts enter the human being from without. One does not form one's own thoughts, but they first enter from the world of archetypal thought. These thoughts change sound into word within the soul, thereby creating self-consciousness. However, owing to this continuous and ever deeper entry of thinking into the human being, the phantom begins to disintegrate under its onslaught.

We now face the primal question with which we started, the posing of which is indeed a daring venture: what is the relation of the phantom to the human I? This is the true Easter question.

What is the connection of the ego – which we are somewhat conscious of, and which runs like a golden thread throughout life from the moment memory begins in the third year – to the human form?

If we look back beyond the present stage of Earth evolution, about which we have just spoken, to the earlier stages of Old Moon, Old Sun and Old Saturn and allow images of those stages to rise within us, then we can say that first the physical body was created by the gods in the primeval conditions of Old Saturn. During the course of the following stage of Earth evolution, that of Old Sun, the forces of life or the ether body were woven into the primal conditions of the physical body. During Old Moon, feelings and sensations entered into this physical-etheric body; nature had by now become one of warmth, light and air. In the developing human form the first inklings of outside and inside awoke, of being related to the divine surrounding and of a dawning, dreamlike consciousness of self, and thereby what became the astral body was incorporated. All this was human form – physical, etheric and astral form – created and evolved over aeons from Old Saturn, Old Sun and Old Moon to the present Earth when the three earlier evolutionary stages were recapitulated once again and shaped into the form of the physical, the living and the sentient that we now know. Only after this form had been created did what we call the human ego begin to descend into it.

Sketch based on blackboard drawing done at the time.

We can divine that the human form developed in the way we tried to outline earlier. The form of a head evolved into the form of a body. You will remember the form that we drew yesterday – it was this that was created. But the human ego remained above it until all was completed. Then the ego entered in and the Divine Thought, which created the Word out of sound, became the human being.

We could perhaps say that the human ego remained above, waiting throughout the whole of creation until the moment during the Atlantean age when the mid-point of Earth evolution had been reached and it could enter into its own; for only because it was itself form could it take up dwelling in its own form, that is, in the human form that had been shaped three times.

Perhaps we could advance a step further and say that in a similar way in which the human ego waited above from the beginning of creation until its form had developed, so also from the beginning of earth evolution a part of that ego that took its dwelling in the human form had remained above. It remained above as the new Adam in order not to go through the Fall, through earthly temptation and earthly destiny. Just as the great ego of humanity waited from the beginning of creation, so the higher brother of the Adam-soul waited from the beginning of Earth evolution, and only at the turning point of time became that child whom the shepherds came and adored.

Following carefully what Rudolf Steiner repeatedly tried to make us understand about this Nathan being, we can note that he described it as the ego, and yet also says that it consisted of only three sheaths – the physical, etheric and astral sheaths into which the other Jesus entered in the twelfth year. From this we might divine that human form, phantom and ego are one and the same but in different guises. The I is created; it is the Word, and it lives as form in the pulse, as word and thought in the breath, and can only realise itself by seeing, by recognising itself in its own mirror and knowing: this is I.

Perhaps this can be a fitting conclusion to our journey along the many paths that we have walked this past week. It is something that Novalis expressed in a similar way when he said that the youth of Sais can only behold the image by tearing away the curtain, but that he then sees

– 'greatest of wonders' – himself! This is, perhaps, a first understanding of what St Paul called the old and the new Adam. Rudolf Steiner called it the phantom, the consumed and the renewed form, and he described how out of that part of the ego that became the Nathan being (which in turn was enlightened and irradiated by the Logos) there can arise what is now renewed for every human being. This is what I wanted to say, but perhaps it is justified to quote one more passage from the Easter lecture of April 2, 1920, in order that Rudolf Steiner has the last word at the end of these considerations:

> The only possible way for people nowadays to have a right feeling about Easter is for them to direct their thoughts to the world catastrophe of our own time. I do not mean only the catastrophe of the recent years of war. I refer to that world catastrophe in which human beings have lost all idea of the connection between the earthly and what is beyond the earth. The time has come when we must realise with full and clear consciousness that supersensible knowledge needs to arise from the grave of our materialistic outlook. For together with supersensible knowledge will arise the knowledge of Christ Jesus. In fact, the only fitting symbol for the Easter festival is that the entire soul-destiny of humanity has been crucified upon the cross of materialism. But humanity itself must do something before there can arise from the grave of human materialism all that can come from supersensible knowledge.[6]

Whit Sunday Address

Newton Dee, June 5, 1960

Dear friends

It was twenty-one years ago today, on Whit Sunday (although the date then was May 28), that a small band of people gathered together in order to open, in a more or less festive way, in the way in which it was possible at that time, a small home for curative education here in Scotland. It was Kirkton House. I thought it justified to mention it because it was, more or less, the conscious beginning of Camphill, or rather the conscious beginning of the curative educational work of Camphill. And that it started on Whit Sunday was not something that was planned or thought out; it just came about that way. Very few of those who were then present are with us here in this room – as far as I can count, only four – but many others have joined us since then. And so I thought, now that we are in the coming-of-age of Camphill, and with it being Whitsun, that it should be mentioned, if only as a passing remark that might be important to some of us but unimportant to others. It was in Kirkton House that this happened.

Much more important, of course, much more pointing towards the future, is all that we tried to gather together at Easter, when we tried to understand what stood behind the Goetheanum, behind the impulse that revealed itself in that remarkable building.[1] In these consecutive talks we were able to paint certain images, consider certain historic streams, meet certain historic personalities, that showed us the impulses that stand behind the Goetheanum. And I remind you how we gradually came to understand that behind the Goetheanum there appeared two historic streams that two thousand years ago were represented on the one hand by the shepherds in the Gospel of St Luke, and on the other by the three Wise Men, the three kings, in the Gospel of St Matthew. And we referred to the lectures that Rudolf Steiner gave at Christmas 1920, where he so openly referred to these two streams.[2] He followed them down into our own time and showed what had become of them, how the stream of the shepherds lost its faith, its inmost being, and thereby developed into all that reveals itself today as natural science, and how the stream of the kings – which had once revealed the images of the cosmos and knew the beinghood of all that lies in the stars and the whole World All – how this stream became in our time mathematics and astronomy. Now the shepherds have disappeared and natural science has appeared; the kings have faded away, leaving behind astronomy, phoronomy and mathematics of our time.

And then we could go one step further and we could, with the help of certain indications from Rudolf Steiner, speak of the two Sophia beings in connection with the stream of the shepherds and the stream of the kings: the Sophia of wisdom, the spirit that once upon a time stood behind the shepherds, and the Sophia being who stood behind the kings. How the latter was dispersed into universal spaces by the power of Lucifer and the other was overcome by Ahriman, who put a paper crown on her head and robbed her of her son Horus (I speak now in these images that we tried to understand at Easter) and how, through the deeds of Ahriman, the spirit of natural science had to serve technology. Many modern methods are the result of this.

But we have followed it one step further. Since the 1920s important developments have come about in the natural sciences as well as in mathematics and astronomy; even the development of medicine was affected. By those developments it has happened that even the last reality – what we would call the materialistic reality as described by natural science, astronomy and mathematics – has disappeared, and in the course of the last twenty years something entirely new has developed. What was still the cell in the organic structure, the molecule in the inorganic structure and the atom itself have dissolved more and more. The atom is no longer an atom, which means something that cannot be divided any more – *atomos* means indivisible. It was found that the atom consisted of many other different parts, and these parts were given names: electrons, protons, neutrons and so on. And even these parts dissolved and are today, for modern physics, nothing more than mathematical formulas. Not even thoughts, just formulas, possibilities, modalities of matter and antimatter (this is a word that is now used), which both in point of fact do not exist. And what until then – until thirty, twenty years ago – was still a thought-out, counted-out cosmos, today has also turned into nothing else but a formula of many formulas. These formulas are understandable to only a very select group of people, but they hold the key to these formulas in their hands and through this, as it were, rob other people not only of understanding but of the certainty of their existence.

What we have today in the formulating of formulas about what one thinks to be the cosmos, and the formulating of the formulas about what is matter and antimatter, they take away all ground of reality, all ground of existence. Many people know that this development in modern thought is paralleled by a similar development in modern art. If you read a book on modern physics or look at a picture of modern painting or see a sculpture that has been created in the last five or six years, you feel as though the ground under your feet has been taken away. I hope you will understand that I do not criticise, but that I only try to describe. But the ground is being taken away from under our feet and because hardly anyone can bear this consciously, people flee into different forms of so-called life and existence. They live in unrealities because these alone seem to give them a world to live in, even though they are usually produced by various kinds of electrical devices, such as television and radio, and other strong destructive powers, when human beings should really be creating realities. All this seems to keep life going, but it has become lifeless.

All this I had to mention in order to ask: what can we do?

On Easter Sunday we pointed to the indication that Rudolf Steiner gave in the lecture wherein he describes the time of Easter in connection with the Archangel Raphael. He also says that if the Goetheanum should stand then every Easter a kind of mystery play should take place, and the main content of this mystery play would be a dialogue between human beings and Raphael. And I may remind you what we thought that this dialogue would contain. We said it seven weeks ago in the following way. Raphael would speak like this:

> You have not only heard of, but have perhaps even learned to practise, the Cosmic Communion. And in the Cosmic Communion there you have pondered about the heavenly deeds that are working into all that is fluid in your body. But you have also been pondering about the heavenly beings who build up the solid substance in you. And you should learn to understand that once upon a time humanity received the communion of bread and wine, but you now receive it through your own effort, by

your own inner strength. In pondering on the heavenly deeds, you renew the fluid within yourself. When you contemplate the heavenly beings you renew the solid substance within yourself. And with this, as a human being, you renew dying nature.

And Raphael would point, in a way which is true to his character, to the modern conditions around us: to the pollution of water, to the decay of plants, to the destruction that human beings have inflicted on the sheaths of the earth. But Raphael would not accuse; instead he would say:

> It depends on you, from within, to renew all of this.

And humans would then say to Raphael:

> But how? In what way can I do it? Can't you see that I am weak within myself? My thoughts are thin, my feelings are numb, my will is lame.

And then Raphael would answer:

> It is on you to read the inscription on the statue of the New Isis, which says to modern humanity: 'I am the human being. I am the past the present and the future: every mortal should lift my veil.' And you can do it, because you have received into your hands that which is the heavenly metamorphosis of the Communion. It has descended to you 360 days after the threefold verses of the Cosmic Communion were spoken as the last words in the Goetheanum.[3] The metamorphosis of these words could again resound as the Foundation Stone verses [in the Christmas Conference 1923/24]. In the Foundation Stone you can revive your willing in beholding the Father-God; you can renew your feeling by uniting

yourself with the Son-God, and you can awaken your thinking in turning towards the Spirit-God. And if you seal this threefold deed by speaking the words concerning the two streams of the Isis-Sophia, about the light that enlightens the minds of the kings and warms the hearts of the shepherds, then the Mediator is with you. You are not alone. You have received this morsel of divine existence, which will lead you between the formula of the non-existent cosmos and the formulas of the dissolved ground of matter. Then you will be able to hold yourself, to carry yourself, in the light of the Son of Man.

These were the words that we experienced as if they had been received directly from Raphael, and which already point to Whitsun because what Raphael points to – the Foundation Stone meditation – is the Whitsun event in our time. It is the beginning of the metamorphosis of that event which is described in the New Testament as the mighty rushing in of wind and the flaming tongues that settled on the heads of the disciples.

This first Whitsun, however, began in the Upper Room on the evening of Maundy Thursday, when Christ shared the bread and wine of the first Communion Service of the Last Supper with his disciples. There he prepared the lives, the whole earthly existence of the Twelve, with bread and wine for what was going to happen to them fifty-one days later. Behind Whitsun there stands the Last Supper. And what had been prepared in that same room on the evening of Maundy Thursday, was fulfilled on the morning of the first Whit Sunday. To the bread and wine was added the mighty rushing wind in which there appeared the cloven tongues of fire. Air and warmth were thus added to what had been prepared through the solid and fluid elements. The humanity of the disciples was held together by the sacrifice of the Christ. The body and the blood of the disciples were kept alive to endure what was to follow: the event of the Mystery of Golgotha, the walking of Christ among them, his ascension, and the deepest sorrow ever to befall any human being. All of this was only possible for the apostles to endure because they were filled with the transubstantiation that the Christ himself had handed on to them. And then this Whitsun miracle occurred.

We can ask ourselves: what was it that appeared within this mighty rushing wind and in the cloven tongues of fire? What was revealed in this sudden transformation, in this sudden Communion, to those few gathered in the Upper Room? One can describe it from many points of view, but one way to describe it is to say: into this sphere of space-existence, which had emanated from the Godhead and through the deeds of human beings had gradually estranged itself from spirit-existence, into this world of space the Christ entered from out of the being of the sun. And not only did he enter, but he left it again through his ascension in order to make what he had done a permanent deed. The mighty rushing wind that entered into the souls of the apostles ten days after Ascension was the infinity of time uniting itself again with space at Whitsun.

As little as we see light – but instead see only what is illuminated by the light – just as little can we behold the reality of time. We represent time to ourselves in spatial images: as the movements of the sun, planets and the stars, and the images of our clocks and watches. These are all spatial arrangements of something that we do not experience directly, in itself as it were. Just as we know about light although we do not behold the light itself, so it is with time: we know about it but do not experience it directly. But the apostles were filled with the reality of time. It was as if an umbilical cord of time once again united humanity to the creative spirit-universe. As long as we develop within the motherly womb, connected through the placenta by the umbilical cord, the embryo or foetus is an image of how space and time and creative eternity can be one. When, during birth, the umbilical cord is cut and the placenta is disposed of, we become spatial entities. But with the first Whitsun, a kind of spiritual umbilical cord was re-established. And what are the flaming tongues, born in on the mighty rushing wind within the reality of time? This is also revealed to us: that the true names of all things and beings appeared. The destructive element of space was overcome and something was restored in this moment that the Acts of the Apostles describes as the people being able to understand each other in their own language. This was because the archetypal language – the true name of all things and beings – was being spoken: and it appeared on the heads, above the heads of the disciples. Within the umbilical cord of time the Logos made its appearance.

This was what happened so long ago. Then, just thirty-seven years ago, the Goetheanum burned down. Through its burning the words of the Cosmic Communion, which Rudolf Steiner had sounded into this building, were lifted up into universal spaces and were returned, 360 days later, in the form of the Foundation Stone meditation. This Foundation Stone is now the new Whitsun event. In the first three verses we have the mighty rushing wind of our time, and in the last, the fourth verse, we have the blazing tongue of fire of our time. But it is not an event that like on the first Whit Sunday was given to a group of specially selected, specially prepared people. Instead it was given freely, and it is up to each human being today to accept it, to either take it or to leave it, to decide for themselves whether or not to renew their own existence in such a way that the eternal names of things and beings may again work within them.

What happened to the disciples? It was a call, dear friends, and by this call consciousness became enhanced in such a way that we can say it is like when the sun rises in the morning and the fog simply disappears. In the same way, our ordinary thoughts disappear under the on-rush of the words of the Foundation Stone. Whether we want them to disappear or whether we want them to remain and for their darkness to be enhanced – this is entirely a personal decision. But with this Foundation Stone something is given to humanity that can only be compared to that moment in the Communion service when the words 'Peace be with you' are spoken, meaning 'May the light of consciousness be heightened in you.' What was dream turns into day consciousness, and what was day consciousness becomes enhanced consciousness. The whole of Whitsun is, year after year, if it is taken and accepted in the right way, a gradual enlightenment, an enhancement of our consciousness wherein our thinking lives. But our ordinary thinking, as far as it is a purely personal thinking, will gradually fade away. A consciousness will then remain that is empty of all subjectivity, but wherein the eternal names of things and beings will reveal themselves. Like a garden that is properly tended, plants grow and fruits ripen. This is why it is so difficult to speak about Whitsun, because it is connected with the unspoken word, the unmanifest light. It is the time that cannot be experienced, but it is also the ever-widening consciousness of the human being – this consciousness that creates a new space for the infinity of time to live within each human being.

Rudolf Steiner once spoke about Whitsun as the festival of the human ego. But it is one of the mysteries of the human ego that it only is when it is not any more. This is the true meaning of *Per Spiritum Sanctum Reviviscimus*: not I, but the Christ in me.

Whitsun Address

Föhrenbühl, May 17, 1964[1]

Dear friends

It is necessary in this day and age that we understand more and more the festivals people celebrate, to get to know them step by step in their spiritual substance and essence so that it becomes possible to celebrate each individual festival in truth again. The tendency of our time is to make all the festivals the same. Christmas and Easter, Michaelmas and St John's Day are all completely confused. And there is also the tendency to ask oneself why the festivals are necessary at all. We can celebrate days off, and we can rest – but why celebrate festivals? That's all terribly exhausting, and as a result they have basically lost their meaning.

If one looks with open eyes at how people celebrate festivals today, then one can certainly say with more or less justification that these festivals – apart from a traditional sense – have lost their real content. And in a context such as ours, which is part of the larger, broader context of anthroposophical spiritual science, it is absolutely necessary to renew the learning of how to celebrate the festivals. This is necessary because we would completely and utterly forget the existence of a spiritual world – we would no longer remember the origin of our own existence – if we ceased to celebrate and understand the reality of festivals.

It is not too much to say, and to say it in all seriousness, that the life of the earth would die if humans ceased to bring renewed celebrations into this life. Becoming and passing away, life and death, they both join hands in the kingdom of nature, but if people stop bringing the celebration of festivals into nature, then all spiritual renewal dies. If no masses were celebrated, if no festivals were held, then, in a few centuries, life would be condemned to be mere machine-like, automatic existence. Humans would have become a mere continuation of the animal kingdom: they would no longer be born, but cast into the world, like animals are; they would not die to be reborn, but perish, like the bodies of animals and the substance of plants.

This is what I wanted to start with so that we may learn to recognise anew that the festivals are not an existence bound to tradition, but that a renewal of all festivals and of each individual festival is necessary. If we neglect to do this, either today or at Easter, at Christmas or for the coming St John's Day and Michaelmas, if no more germination points of spiritual existence are planted in earthly existence, and if festivals are not named, recognised and celebrated in their true sense, then the connection to the spiritual world ceases. Many of us are involved in this attempt at renewal and have gradually learned to see that every Christmas festival is different from the previous ones, every Easter has a different character, and every Whitsun a different colour, because a festival is a powerful, comprehensive, essential thing in itself. It changes from one year to the next, is different from one region of the earth to another, and changes according to what people do with it and how they celebrate it. So today we want to try to understand from a very specific point of view what Whitsun can mean to us this year.

One can point to something that is more generally valid and that is that the three great Christian festivals of the year, Christmas, Easter and Whitsun, are embedded in a very specific way in the becoming of humanity. They are embedded in the course of time. One can point out with a certain degree of certainty that Christmas is a festival of the past. From ancient times, one can almost say from the beginnings of the development of humanity, the Christmas festival protrudes into the existence of humankind. From this comprehensive past it forms a seed for the future. When we celebrate Christmas in the right way, we feel surrounded, enveloped by everything that once was the human past. You can describe this schematically by saying: here is the seed of the future of Christmas, but it is clothed in the past.

It is equally understandable and unambiguous to say that Easter is essentially a celebration of the present. One must always try to bring the mystery of Golgotha to life in oneself so that Easter can come alive. One must stand before the cross, one must suffer with the disciples, one must go to the tomb with the women. And, when the stone is rolled away, one has to experience the shuddering and the doubt, the longing and then the incomprehension of the disciples when they later see the Risen One in their midst in the Cenacle. This is what is always new and present about Easter in human experience.

And you will understand when I say that Whitsun is the festival of the future. A festival that wants to become, that *is* coming, though it is still barely comprehended by us and our earthly minds.

When we look at all this, perhaps we can sense the deep connection that exists between Christmas and Whitsun, between what has once been and what is to come. Both belong to infinity and this infinity connects Christmas and Whitsun. Today I can only point to a few things that melt together with this past and future as if in a unity.

Christmas	Easter	Whitsun
Past	Present	Future
	Infinity	

Those of you who are familiar with the vestments used at the altars of The Christian Community at Christmas and Whitsun will remember that it is precisely the white chasuble that the priest wears at Whitsun as well as at Christmas. A future light from the past and a past light into the future shines over these two festivals. And once we consider this, we immediately remember how both festivals are birth festivals, and that these two birth festivals are intimately connected with the working of what we so commonly call the Holy Spirit. If we recall, the baby Jesus of Matthew's Gospel, the Solomon Jesus, is proclaimed by the Holy Spirit. He is called to grow and become in his mother's womb by the power of the Holy Spirit. The same happens with the other baby Jesus, the one of Luke's Gospel, the so-called Nathan Jesus. Here, too, the angel appears and announces to Mary that the Holy Spirit has come over her and that a child is now arising in her through the power of the Holy Spirit.

So it is also with the third in the alliance: with John the Baptist. He is begotten, called and formed also by the Holy Spirit to the elderly Elizabeth and her still older husband. And so the Solomon child is born. Then the Mary of Luke's Gospel and Elizabeth meet each other in the time of their pregnancy. At the moment of their meeting they are filled with the Holy Spirit and out of them comes – speaking through them – the angelic greeting, that wonderful word begotten out of the stars that sounds from their mouths.

And that is Christmas. Three children, born one after the other. The Solomon Jesus, of whom Matthew's Gospel speaks; John, who later becomes the Baptist, and the Nathan child, of whom Luke's Gospel speaks.

At the same time, however, individual groups of people are also called by the Holy Spirit. Thus the magi are called by the passage of the stars; they are filled, so to speak, by the Holy Spirit through the passage of the stars. They come to the Solomon child. The shepherds hear the singing of the Holy Spirit and it leads them to the Nathan child. All of this is Christmas. There the Holy Spirit speaks, begets, sings, works through the bodies of the three mothers: the two Marys and the one Elizabeth. The Holy Spirit also speaks to the shepherds and reveals itself to the kings. In this way, what is to take place at the turn of time is prepared.

The two Jesus children become one after their twelfth year. Then, thirty years after the nativity, the Holy Spirit appears again, but now as the dove that descends on Jesus at his baptism by John in the Jordan. Matthew's Gospel says there – and the other Gospels express it in a somewhat similar way:

> And when Jesus was baptised, he went up straightaway
> out of the water, and behold, the heavens were opened
> upon him, and he saw the Spirit of God descending like a
> dove and coming upon him.

The Spirit of God, that is the Holy Spirit. And then it goes on to say:

> And behold a voice from heaven said, 'This is my
> beloved Son, in whom I am well pleased.'

From now on, it is no longer John who baptises with water, but Christ himself with the Holy Spirit. This is all Christmas, because the baptism takes place at the end of the Holy Nights on Epiphany, the day of the three kings, January 6.

If you follow this step by step and piece by piece, these images of life that were woven into the effectiveness of human existence on earth by the hands of the Holy Spirit, and if you try to transform these images from the first Christmas to the first Whitsun and look at one and the other at the same time, then you see the loss that has taken place. By the time of the first Whitsun the Solomon child is gone: he died in his twelfth year. Gone is John the Baptist: he was beheaded when he was thirty years old. Gone is the Nathan child who went through the Mystery of Golgotha. The elderly Elizabeth, who had certainly died by then, has gone. The mother of the Nathan child has also gone, for she died when her own son was about twelve years old.

Who has remained? Only one has remained on earth: the mother of the Solomon child. She carries through the whole process here on earth and now stands in the circle of the twelve disciples at Whitsun. The others have all passed away from the earth.

But the mother of the Nathan child has united spiritually with the Solomon mother. John the Baptist is resurrected in John the Evangelist. And when we ask, 'What happened to the Solomon child? What happened to the Nathan child?', they are also there at Whitsun, only again in spiritual form. When I say this, I mean that they only become visible to the disciples at a very specific time. For the essence of Zarathustra had united with the shell, the etheric shell, of the Solomon Jesus, and the essence of the Buddha had united with the essence of the Nathan child. And these two, they are the two beings in white garments who appear to the disciples on the Mount of Olives after the Christ has left them. Pointing to him who had ascended to heaven, they said to the disciples:

> Men of Galilee, why do you stand here looking up to heaven? This Jesus, who is taken up from you into heaven, shall come again as you have seen him, and shall ascend into heaven.

Thus, clothed in white – that is, filled with spirit being – the two Jesus children stand there again, flanking the Ascension of the Christ.

Then follows the ten days of mourning, abandonment and pain of the disciples. They are united in the Cenacle; Mary comes to them and stays with them. There then occurs what we should remember every Whitsun: the Holy Spirit begins to speak again. This we have to try and imagine: the Holy Spirit begins to speak! For the disciples and all the apostles this had not happened before to the extent that it is happening now. For the Holy Spirit first led, begat and enacted deeds; now it fills individual human beings. And through being filled with the Holy Spirit a powerful thing occurs that we can call the inner Whitsun, the first Pentecost: human beings reach a new level of self-recognition.

It might seem hard to imagine that the apostles and the disciples, even though they were once initiates and walked beside the Christ in the light of his sun, basically did not know it. But it is true. In the end they deny him – yes, all of them, not only Peter. For the others are no longer there when he is condemned, when he is led up to Golgotha, when he is crucified. They have all disappeared because they do not know what is taking place. They doubt the Risen One. They feel the truth in their hearts and yet they cannot recognise it. Only on Whitsun morning, when the rushing wind from heaven sounds and as the new Holy Spirit fills them, do the scales fall from their eyes and they begin to discern and understand. Now they speak with courage of that which before had only been blinding and binding them.

This was prepared through all that which today, looking back into history, we may call Greek philosophy. The Jewish Shavuot festivals, the annual Feast of Weeks on which the first Christian Pentecost took place, were also being prepared. The preparation happened in Greece through Plato and Aristotle. This was then taken up by Paul after the Mystery of Golgotha and was transformed into the Pentecostal message to the Areopagus Assembly in Athens. It became what we can call the first Christian mystery school, that of Dionysius the Areopagite.[2] This was none other than Paul himself. This Pentecostal teaching continued to propagate, going underground in the fourth and fifth centuries so that it can be resurrected in our time.

Thus Whitsun gradually submerged itself into the life of humanity. The whole of philosophy, from the Church Fathers through the ninth and tenth centuries, on into the twelfth, thirteenth and fourteenth centuries with the nominalists and realists, up to the modern philosophy of the eighteenth and nineteenth centuries – all of this in the end originated from the first Whitsun event. All of this is an attempt to develop self-knowledge. Whether it is Descartes or de la Mettrie, Hegel, Fichte or Kant, it is always an attempt to understand oneself out of the Pentecostal spirit. And even if it was watered down, it was out of this Pentecostal spirit that consciousness grew; that is, the knowledge of oneself as a human being. This came to an end in the course of the nineteenth century. It was the end of the first philosophy: that of Plato, Aristotle and the first Dionysius-Paul. The philosophy of the first Pentecost came to an end at that moment when Rudolf Steiner began to write a new epistemology based on Pauline Christianity and which he set down in *The Philosophy of Freedom*. From then on, there were many attempts at a renewal of philosophy. Rudolf Steiner's attempt, however, grew far beyond an attempt in that it became a new revelation.

But if you really try to understand modern philosophy – real philosophy such as that of Scheler, Jaspers and many other important great philosophers – you will notice that something completely new is beginning. If you read Heidegger, study Husserl, and go along with Scheler's thought formations, you will get the sense that a new Holy Spirit is stirring: namely, the one that can be addressed in *The Philosophy of Freedom*. What is this all about? One can express it in other ways, but in this context I would like to express it simply as the human being developing towards what one can call the spiritual communion, the Cosmic Communion.

That which the young Rudolf Steiner described in one of his first writings on Goethe's world view, as apprehending the idea in reality, is the true communion of the human being. This is where a new Christianity begins, where a new understanding of human self-knowledge begins, and where anthroposophy begins as the new Pentecostal event.

At Christmas – because it could not be otherwise – on December 31, 1922, he said:

> Thoughts that we make in our ordinary knowledge of Nature – thoughts about that which is dying away – are mere reflections, not realities. But thoughts we receive from spiritual research are quickened in Imagination, Inspiration, and Intuition. If we accept them they become forms having independent existence in the life of the Earth.
>
> Concerning these creative thoughts, I once said in my book entitled *A Theory of Knowledge Implicit in Goethe's World Conception*, that such thinking represents the spiritual form of communion among humanity. For as long as human beings gives themselves up to their mirror-thoughts about external Nature, they do nothing but repeat the past. They live in corpses of the divine.

> When they bring life into their thoughts, then, giving and receiving communion through their own being, they ally themselves with the element of divine spirit that permeates the world and assures its future.³

Hear the Pentecostal call from these words: experiencing communion with the divine-spiritual that permeates the world and assures its future! Thus spiritual knowledge is the real communion, the beginning of a cosmic ritual appropriate to humanity in the present age. It can come into being through humans becoming aware of how they permeate their physical-mineral and their vegetable organism. How, by enlivening the spirit within themselves, they now also bring the spirit into that which otherwise surrounds them as dead and dying. And this is what Rudolf Steiner draws our attention to in these lectures.

I have already said at the beginning of this lecture that the earthly and the vegetative (we could also say the physical and etheric), which manifest themselves in solid and fluid, is effective in earthly existence. The form of the stars flows into the earthly, into the physical, in such a way that they are given to us as images in matter. In Rudolf Steiner's lecture to which I have just referred, he goes on to say:

> With the substance of the Earth that is contained in Earth-activity, we take into us the being of the stars, the being of the heavens. But we must be conscious that we as human beings, by a deliberate, loving act of human will, transform that which has become matter, back again into spirit. In this manner we perform a real act of transubstantiation. We become aware of our own part in the world and so the spiritual thought-life is quickened within us.

And in connection with this Rudolf Steiner spoke the following verse:

> In Earth-activity draws near to me,
> Given to me in substance-imaged form,
> The Heavenly Being of the Stars.
> In Willing I see them transformed with Love!

He then adds that that which we take into our fluid organism, which is connected with the blood circulation, does not flow from the realm of the fixed stars, but from the sphere of the planets. They are the paths of the stars, that is, the deeds of the stars. And the corresponding formula is:

> In Watery life stream into me,
> Forming me through with power of substance-force,
> The Heavenly Deeds of the Stars –
> In Feeling I see them transformed with Wisdom!

These mantric lines, which indeed suggest a cosmic communion for the human being – the daily communion that happens with and for all of us – point to the duality of bread and wine and at the same time to the duality of shepherds and kings.

The loving will was once alive in the shepherds. It was the ancient knowledge of nature that saw the archetypes of all existence with loving devotion. Loving devotion has disappeared from these imaginings, and natural science, based on experiment and one-sided observation, has developed from them. It has gone on to degrade human beings to the level of the animal.

The Nathan being alone, who carries the spirit of the Buddha within itself, can renew this knowledge of nature that has fallen from its path.

The former astronomical knowledge of the magi, the three kings, which was born of wise, knowing feeling, has disappeared. Their inspirations have become abstract mathematics and phoronomy. From it arose the present-day calculation and speculation of modern physics, and through it the disintegrating and destructive powers that rule within matter have been set free.

The Solomon child alone, bearing the spirit of Zarathustra, can bring healing renewal.

Human beings degraded to the level of the animal, and the unleashing of the forces of nature surrounding them, which threaten the true human image because they seek to destroy it – this is the image of our epoch. We cannot close our eyes to it. We now carry the responsibility for calling up the healing forces within us that may once again become a blessing for humanity.

Once more the two Jesus children rise up before us: the Nathan and the Solomon beings. The child of shepherd simplicity, the child of loving will; and the child of the magi, the child of wise and knowing feeling.

But now they stand before us as the two men looking down on us humans from the Mount of Olives. Yes, we are like the disciples on the first Ascension Day, for the Christ has also disappeared from us. Forsaken, we stand there and look upwards, if we still have the strength to lift our eyes to the Mount of Olives, to the spirit. If we do, the two white-robed figures appear; but they do not say today what they spoke to the disciples then. When we hear their voices, we hear the words:

> People, why do you stand gazing into the world of the senses? The Christ has appeared in the clouds of heaven and is already revealing himself today to souls who want to create a new Pentecost within themselves.

This is the call that rings out to us today. We should try and hear it! The verses of the cosmic communion prepare us to hear this voice. That is why Rudolf Steiner says in the lecture already mentioned:

What would otherwise be mere abstract knowledge achieves a relationship of will and feeling to the world. The world becomes the temple, the house of God. When we, as knowing beings, summon up our powers of will and feeling, we become sacrificing beings. Our fundamental relationship to the world rises from knowledge to cosmic ritual.

The first beginning of what must come to pass if Anthroposophy is to fulfil its mission in the world is that our whole relationship to the world must be recognised to be one of cosmic ritual or cult.

Soon after these words were spoken, the Goetheanum went up in the flames, the blaze lighting up the New Year's night of 1922–23. It disappeared for the eyes of the people as the Christ disappeared for the eyes of the disciples.

But the message of the Holy Spirit reached us when the words of the Foundation Stone meditation entered our hearts. In these mantras the transfigured body of the being of anthroposophy appears. It reveals itself between the two men in white robes on the Mount of Olives in our time. Thus Whitsun becomes the festival of this epoch of humanity, and Whitsun becomes the festival of anthroposophy. For this being – a being transfigured in form, appearing between the two Jesus children who are permeated and filled with the spirit of Buddha and the essence of Zarathustra – now proclaims the return of Christ in the etheric kingdom of the earth. It is the living message of a World Pentecost: that is the mission of ever enlivened spiritual science, of the ever-widening spirit-knowledge, which is a cosmic cultus! This is what I wanted to express this evening.

Notes

Karl König and the Festivals
1. See *Karl König: My Task*.
2. See *The Spirit of Camphill*, Floris Books, 2018, and *Plays for the Festivals of the Year*, Floris Books, 2017.
3. See also *Karl König and Kaspar Hauser*, Floris Books, UK 2012, and Peter Selg, *Ita Wegman and Karl König: Letters and Documents*, Floris Books, UK 2008.
4. See endnote 1 above. The event of the opening of Kirkton House is also spoken of in the address for Whitsun 1960, included in this book.
5. See the two volumes of Karl König's works: *An Inner Journey Through the Year* and *The Calendar of the Soul*, both published by Floris Books in 2010.
6. The address is given in full in this volume.
7. From unpublished reports, Camphill Archive, Aberdeen.
8. Rudolf Steiner, *Study of Man* (CW293), Rudolf Steiner Press, UK 2011.
9. In *The Cycle of the Year as Breathing-Process of the Earth* (GA223). Lecture of April 1, 1923.
10. From a letter to Carlo Pietzner. See *The Spirit of Camphill*, p. 24.
11. Karl König, *Plays for the Festivals of the Year*, Floris Books 2017.
12. The whole poem is contained in *Stories, Meditations and Poems*, Floris Books, UK 2020, p. 116f

The Human Being and the Festivals of the Year
Translated from the German by G. S. Francis. A lecture given in May, 1932, at the Curative Education Home, Schloss Pilgramshein, Silesia. Reprinted from *Anthroposophy* Vol. 1 No.4 Christmas 1932.
1. Particularly in the lectures contained in *The Cycle of the Year as Breathing-Process of the Earth* (GA223).
2. Contained in *The Archangel Michael – His Mission and Ours*, Anthroposophic Press, USA 1994.

The Human Being and the Cycle of the Year

First published in the Calendar, Easter 1933–1934, of the Section for Mathematics and Astronomy at the Goetheanum, Dornach. Translated from the German by Tascha Babitch.

The Year as a Living Being

1. *The Four Seasons and the Archangels* (CW229), Rudolf Steiner Press, UK 2008. Lecture of October 12, 1923.
2. See 'The Last Address', contained in *Karmic Relationships, Volume 4* (CW238), Rudolf Steiner Press, UK 1997.
3. The light can be very strong in that area of Scotland and, being so far north, the night is very short during the summer.
4. Refers to a Rosicrucian mantra given by Rudolf Steiner. See *Freemasonry and Ritual Work* (CW265), SteinerBooks, USA 2007, pp. 172 and 284f.
5. A Rosicrucian fairy tale from Scene Five of *The Soul's Probation*, the second of Rudolf Steiner's four Mystery Dramas. See *Four Mystery Dramas* (CW14), Steiner Books, USA 2007, p.53f.
6. Karl König's previous lecture in Camphill was on June 5, 1963 and was the last of a series of six lectures, starting on May 26th, about the life and work of Rudolf Steiner. These lectures are in the Karl König Archive but have not yet been published.
7. *Verses and Meditations*, Rudolf Steiner Press, UK 2004, p. 97.

Individual and Historic Conscience

1. Ehrenfried Pfeiffer had lived in the community in Spring Valley, New York, since 1948. He died on November 30, 1961, between the two summer conferences that König helped to organise there in 1960 and 1962.
2. See *Anthroposophical Leading Thoughts* (CW26), Rudolf Steiner Press, UK 2007, p. 201f.
3. *The Four Seasons and the Archangels*, lecture of October 12, 1923.
4. *East in the Light of the West* (CW113), Rudolf Steiner Press, UK 2017, lecture of August 24, 1909. See also *Transforming the Soul: Volume 2* (CW59), Rudolf Steiner Press, UK 2006, lectures of May 5 and 12, 1910.
5. The series of moon nodes (crossing the ecliptic of the sun) move in a clockwise direction around the zodiac and take 18 years, 7 months and 9 days to make one complete revolution. This can be seen as a significant time rhythm for biographic or historic events. König was always aware of such cosmic rhythms.

NOTES

6. Karl Jaspers published his book *Existenzphilosophie* in 1938. It was translated into English in 1971 as *Philosophy of Existence* by the University of Pennsylvania Press.
7. *The Four Seasons and the Archangels*, p. 50.

A Michaelmas Lecture, 1965

Translated by Richard Steel.

1. See the Michaelmas lectures König gave in *Becoming Human: A Social Task*, Floris Books, UK 2011.
2. Contained in *Festivals and their Meaning*, Rudolf Steiner Press, UK 2002, p. 383f.
3. The festive opening of the first Camphill Village in central Europe, the Lehenhof, was on September 25, 1965, and the days around that were celebrated as part of the Michaelmas festival with many visitors.
4. Georg and Erika von Arnim were the founders of the Camphill school Föhrenbühl. Georg (1920–2000) had been part of the medical group with Karl König in Scotland and became König's personal physician during his last years after his move to Lake Constance.
5. Schweitzer was criticised because of his alleged support of colonialism and racism. The American journalist John Gunther visited Lambaréné in the 1950s and reported Schweitzer's patronising attitude towards Africans.
6. See *Martin Buber: A Life of Faith and Dissent*, by Paul Mendes-Flohr, Yale University Press, USA 2019.
7. The priest in question was Otto Palmer. When he told Rudolf Steiner that he wanted to become a priest of the Christian Community Steiner said, "Well you will have to occupy yourself for at least two years with Baal Schem." Steiner suggested that Otto Palmer use Martin Buber as a key to enter into a world he knew nothing about. Before Baruch Urieli had become a priest, König advised him to research into the same theme, commenting on an inner connection between Baal Shem and Count Zinzendorf. (See Baruch Urieli; "Zur Mission des Baal Shem Tov" in the "Pfarrer-Rundbrief" of the Christian Community, September 1981.)
8. Rabbi Israel ben Eliezer (1698–1760), Ukrainian Jewish healer and mystic and founder of Hasidic Judaism.
9. Present-day Hasidism is a sub-group within Haredi ('ultra-Orthodox') Judaism. König seems to have considered the founding of the ultra-Orthodox organization Agudath Israel in Poland in

1912 to have been the end of the mystic Hasidic movement as a spiritual revivalist impulse. Apart from significant opposition within Judaism beginning already at the end of the eighteenth century, the movement was then strongly decimated by the Eastern European pogroms of the nineteenth and early twentieth centuries, and particularly by the Holocaust.

10. That is probably where the story 'The Idle Tongue' came from that König later wrote down. It is included in the book *Stories, Poems and Meditations,* Floris Books, 2020.
11. Originally published in German, in 1922, the English translation was published in 1924. The first chapter 'How I Came to be a Doctor in the Forest' begins with the words quoted.
12. It is certainly not unrelated that Karl König mentions the Michaelmas festivities at the Lehenhof in the first part of this lecture. There, for the address at the opening of this first Village Community in central Europe, he had spoken in a very special way about the 'silent steam' running through history. His address is printed in the biography *Karl König* by Hans Müller-Wiedemann, Camphill Books 1996. See also the introduction to *The Spirit of Camphill,* Floris Books, UK 2018, pp. 28–29.
13. *Wonders of the World, Trials of the Soul, Revelations of the Spirit* (CW129), Rudolf Steiner Press, UK 2020, pp. 7–8.
14. The Thirty Years' War lasted from 1618– 648.
15. In the volume *At the Threshold of the Modern Age,* biographies of twenty-four further personalities have been compiled that König also describes in relation to the dawning of the Michael Age.
16. König had written a series of three essays for the periodical *Die Kommenden* in 1963 and given two public lectures in Stuttgart on the Thalidomide scandal. The essays were then printed as a booklet in German and the two lectures translated into English. As yet they have not been published.
17. Unfortunately only few letters are in the Karl König Archive. Schweitzer was connected to the start of Camphill in America and gave his name as patron for the first years of Camphill Village Copake (see *Karl König in America,* self-published by the Karl König Institute, Berlin, 2020).
18. *Reincarnation and Karma: Their Significance in Modern Culture* (CW135), Anthroposophic Press, USA 1960.
19. *Karmic Relationships: Volume 4* (CW238), p. 172.

NOTES

On the Significance of the Twelve Holy Days

1. The words of the Archangel Raphael from J. W. Goethe's *Faust – Part One*, 'Prologue in the Heavens'.

New Year's Eve Address, 1965–66

1. The previous year, Karl König had described the connection between Mars and the beginning of the Rosicrucian work on earth. At the same time, in 1604, the being of Buddha received a new task within the spiritual sphere of Mars. Particularly in the lecture on December 18, 1912, Rudolf Steiner had spoken about the 'cosmic sacrifice' that the spirit being of Buddha performed in the seventeenth century, to take his impulse of peace into the warlike realm of Mars – a deed similar to Christ's deed for the earth.
2. In March of that year, 1966, Karl König died due to his heart condition. It is perhaps of significance that he foresaw this particular melody of the stars leading up to March.
3. The Foundation Stone of the Anthroposophical Society, given by Rudolf Steiner during the Christmas Conference of 1923–24 in Dornach. On the morning of December 25, Rudolf Steiner spoke in a deeply moving way of the Foundation Stone as a 'stone of love, which today we will lower into our hearts'. (GA260). Karl König read the words of the Foundation Stone each year for the New Year's celebration, and this became a tradition in many Camphill communities around the world.

The 'Entry into Jerusalem'

Translated by Richard Steel.

The Experience of Easter Within the Human Being

1. From *Faust – Part One*, 'Outside the City Gate'.
2. König has probably made his own translation. The usual translation is: 'In vain the Cross of Golgotha was raised – thou hast not any part in its deliverance unless it be raised up within thy heart.' From 'Inwardness', contained in *The Cherubinic Wanderer*.
3. In the Karlstejn castle. See also Karl König, *Becoming Human: A Social Task*, Floris Books, 2011 for lectures and drawings about the castle.

World Breath and World Pulse

The following four lectures were given by Karl König for Easter 1965 in the Camphill School community Föhrenbühl in Germany.
1. From *Faust – Part One*, 'Outside the City Gate'.
2. A. C. Harwood, for instance, used the term 'bliss of growth'.

Human Breath and Human Pulse

1. Verses from the *Calendar of the Soul* were performed in eurythmy.
2. Steiner, Rudolf, *From Jesus to Christ* (CW131), Rudolf Steiner Press, UK 1991, p. 101.
3. Karl König had given a series of five lectures and a New Year's address called 'Man as a Social Being and the Mission of Conscience'. These were printed under this title by Camphill Press in 1990.
4. Steiner, Rudolf, *The Inner Being of Man and Our Life Between Death and Rebirth* (CW153), Rudolf Steiner Press, UK 2013, p. 80.

Easter, the Festival of Resurrection

1. *From Jesus to Christ*, p. 113.
2. Ibid. p. 127f.
3. From notes taken by Elisabeth Vreede in *From the History and the Contents of the First Section of the Esoteric School, 1904–14* (CW264), SteinerBooks, USA 2007, pp. 193–203.
4. *From Jesus to Christ*, p. 128f.
5. Steiner, Rudolf, *The Gospel of St Mark* (CW139), Anthroposophic Press, USA 1986, p. 175f.
6. *From Jesus to Christ*, p. 145.
7. See *Approaching the Mystery of Golgotha*, lecture of June 1, 1914.

Earthly Creation, Human Form and Human Ego

1. *The Festivals and their Meaning*, p. 135f.
2. *From Jesus to Christ*, p. 143f.
3. Steiner, Rudolf, *The Riddle of Humanity* (CW170), Rudolf Steiner Press, UK 1990, p. 204.
4. Steiner, Rudolf, *Good and Evil Spirits and Their Influence on Humanity* (CW102), Rudolf Steiner Press, UK 2014, p. 60.
5. Ibid. p. 68.
6. *The Festivals and their Meaning*, p. 137f.

NOTES

Whit Sunday Address

1. For Easter 1960, Karl König had given a series of three lectures about the Goetheanum in connection to the Grail (first lecture), to the 'New Isis' (second lecture), and the individuality of Raphael (third lecture).
2. See *The Search for the New Isis, the Divine Sophia* (CW202), Mercury Press, USA 1983.
3. On December 31, 1922, Rudolf Steiner had given an address in the Goetheanum called 'The Threefold Human Being and the Cycle of the Year – the Cosmic Communion of Humanity'. Immediately after the last visitors had left the building, the night watchman noticed smoke. It wasn't long before the Goetheanum was consumed by flames.

Whitsun Address

Translated from the German by Cornelius Bruhn.
1. On Ascension Day, May 7, 1964, Karl König had officially opened the Camphill School Community at Föhrenbühl with a talk.
2. Karl König had given a series of lectures about this two years previously. They are published in the volume *The Grail and the Development of Conscience: St. Paul and Parsifal*, Floris Books, 2016.
3. This and further quotes are from *Man and the World of Stars: The Spiritual Communion of Mankind* (CW219), Anthroposophic Press, US 1963.

Bibliography

Jaspers, Karl, *Philosophy of Existence*, University of Pennsylvania Press, USA 1971.
König, Karl, *An Inner Journey Through the Year*, Floris Books, UK 2010.
—, *At the Threshold of the Modern Age: Biographies Around the Year 1861*, Floris Books, UK 2011.
—, *Becoming Human: A Social Task*, Floris Books, UK 2011.
—, *The Calendar of the Soul*, Floris Books, UK 2010.
—, *The Grail and the Development of Conscience: St Paul and Parsifal*, Floris Books, UK 2016.
—, *Karl König and Kaspar Hauser*, Floris Books, UK 2012.
—, *Karl König: My Task*, Floris Books, UK 2008.
—, *Plays for the Festivals of the Year*, Floris Books, UK 2017.
—, *The Spirit of Camphill: Birth of a Movement*, Floris Books, UK 2018.
—, *Stories, Meditations and Poems*, Floris Books, UK 2020.
Mendes-Flohr, Paul, *Martin Buber: A Life of Faith and Dissent*, Yale University Press, USA 2019.
Selg, Peter, *Ita Wegman and Karl König: Letters and Documents*, Floris Books, UK 2008.
Steiner, Rudolf. Volume Nos refer to the Collected Works (CW) or to the German Gesamtausgabe (GA).
—, *Anthroposophical Leading Thoughts* (CW26), Rudolf Steiner Press, UK 2007.
—, *Approaching the Mystery of Golgotha* (CW152), SteinerBooks, USA 2006.

—, *The Cycle of the Year as Breathing-Process of the Earth* (GA223), Anthroposophic Press, USA 1984.
—, *East in the Light of the West* (CW113), Rudolf Steiner Press, UK 2017.
—, *The Festivals and their Meaning*, Rudolf Steiner Press, UK 2002.
—, *Four Mystery Dramas* (CW14), Steiner Books, USA 2007.
—, *The Four Seasons and the Archangels* (CW229), Rudolf Steiner Press, UK 2008.
—, *From Jesus to Christ* (CW131), Rudolf Steiner Press, UK 1991.
—, *Good and Evil Spirits and Their Influence on Humanity* (CW102), Rudolf Steiner Press, UK 2014.
—, *The Gospel of St Mark* (CW139), Anthroposophic Press, USA 1986.
—, *The Inner Being of Man and Our Life Between Death and Rebirth* (CW153), Rudolf Steiner Press, UK 2013.
—, *Karmic Relationships, Volume 4* (CW238), Rudolf Steiner Press, UK 1997.
—, *Man and the World of Stars: The Spiritual Communion of Mankind* (CW219), Anthroposophic Press, USA 1963.
—, *Reincarnation and Karma: Their Significance in Modern Culture* (CW135), Anthroposophic Press, USA 1960.
—, *The Riddle of Humanity* (CW170), Rudolf Steiner Press, UK 1990.
—, *The Study of Man* (CW293), Rudolf Steiner Press, UK 2011.
—, *Transforming the Soul: Volume 2* (CW59), Rudolf Steiner Press, UK 2006.
—, *Verses and Meditations*, Rudolf Steiner Press, UK 2004.
—, *Wonders of the World, Trials of the Soul, Revelations of the Spirit* (CW129), Rudolf Steiner Press, UK 2020.

Index

Aeschylus 58
Aquinas, Thomas 62
Aristotle 185
ash 157f, 164f
astronomy 170f
autumn, correspondence with blood vessels 30

Baal Shem Tov (Rabbi Israel ben Eliezer) 73f
blood iron, correspondence with Michaelmas 34
blood vessels, correspondence with autumn 30
bones, correspondence with winter 27
breath 128f, 144
—, as death process 131, 141, 158f
Buber, Martin 69f, 74f, 78f
Buddha 183, 188

Calendar of the Soul 117–24
carbon 156f
carbon dioxide process 40f
Christ 147f, 175
—, Etheric 102

Christmas 25, 93f, 96, 180f
—, correspondence with larynx 32
conscience
—, development of 58f
—, historic 47, 57f, 61
—, individual 57f
cosmic breath 163f
Cosmic Communion 172f, 176, 186f
cosmic intelligence 60f
cosmic pulse 163f
cosmic will 63
cycle of the year 51f

diamond 156f
Dionysius the Areopagite 185

Earth evolution 162
Earth soul 38, 40
Easter 25, 116f, 139f, 154, 180
—, correspondence with heart 32
ego–consciousness 135f, 143f
Eliezer, Rabbi Israel ben (Baal Shem Tov) 73f
Elijah 59
Epiphany 93f, 96f

Erinyes 58
Etheric Christ 102
Euripides 58f

Fall, the 135, 142f
festivals, as spiritual senses of the Earth 22f
Foundation Stone meditation 173f, 176f, 190

Goetheanum 170
Golgotha, Mystery of 137, 152
Greek philosophy 185

Hasidism 73f, 77
heart 43, 131, 162
—, correspondence with Easter 32
Hercules 136
Herrnhuter Brotherhood 73f
historic conscience 47, 57f, 61
Holy Days and Nights 91f
Holy Spirit, the 181f, 190
hydrogen process 43

Jairus' daughter 136, 145f, 160
Yahweh 59, 116, 158
John the Baptist 181f
Jupiter 94f, 96

karma 54, 80f
kidneys 42f

Lazarus 136f, 146f, 160
larynx, correspondence with Christmas 32
liver 41f
lungs 40f

mathematics 170f, 189

Michael (archangel) 60f, 83
—, Age of 78, 81
Michaelmas 25, 66f
—, correspondence with blood iron 34
muscles, correspondence with spring 27
Mystery of Golgotha 137, 152

Nain, youth of 136f, 146, 160
Nathan Jesus 148f, 167f, 181f, 188
natural science 170f, 188
nerves, correspondence with summer 29
New Year's Eve 93, 97f
nitrogen process 42f

Old Moon 165f
Old Saturn 165f
Old Sun 95, 165f
Orestes 58
oxygen process 40f

Paul, St 131f, 185
Persephone 38
phantom (spirit-germ) 134, 140f, 148f, 156f, 165
Philosophy of Freedom, The 185f
pietism 74, 77
pineal gland 162
—, correspondence with St John's tide 33
Plato 185
Pluto 38
Prometheus 135f
pulse 128f, 144
—, as enlivening 131

Raphael (archangel) 48f, 172f
'rapture of becoming' (*Werdelust*) 119f, 124f

INDEX

—, as world I 122
resurrection 151f
Rosicrucianism 77f, 153

St Germain, Count 77
St John's tide 25, 51f, 117
—, correspondence with pineal gland 33
Saturn 93f, 96
Schweitzer, Albert 69, 71f, 74f, 78f
seasons-plant 39, 44
Solomon Jesus 148, 181f, 189
solstice, winter 91
Son of Man 151f
spirit-germ (phantom) 134, 140f, 148f, 156f, 165
spring, correspondence with muscles 28
staretsdom 74f, 77
summer
—, as out-breathing 20f
—, correspondence with nerves 29

Thirty Years' War 77
time 175f

Uriel (archangel) 47, 53, 59, 61, 63f
Urpflanze 39

Werdelust ('rapture of becoming') 119f, 124f
Whitsun 174f, 180f, 184f, 190
winter
—, as in-breathing 20f
—, correspondence with bones 27
— solstice 91
world I 122

Zarathustra 183, 189
Zeus 96
Zinzendorf, Ludwig Count 73

You may also be interested in...

Before Birth and Beyond Death

The Transformation of the Human Being

Karl König

In these important lectures and essays, König argues that the greatest part of our community exists beyond this earthly life. He calls on us not to neglect our connection with them and encourages us to solicit their guidance so that we might rediscover the values that our society has lost.

König suggests that by changing our everyday thinking, we can create a bridge across the threshold of death, allowing essential communication between humans in different states of being and uniting humankind to the benefit of all.

florisbooks.co.uk

Plays for the Festivals of the Year

Karl König

Karl König's plays for the festivals of the year are arguably his most original creations. Written to be performed in Camphill communities, they show a deep understanding of the Christian festivals.

With one exception, all fourteen plays were written during the early years of the Camphill movement, and König's hope was that their performance would help bring communities together. Not only is their content entertaining and informative, but the act of performing provides great benefits as social therapy. and other communities around the world.

This is the first time that the original texts of all the plays have been published together. They are presented with an introduction and commentary by series editor Richard Steel, alongside fascinating performance photographs.

florisbooks.co.uk

*A selection of books in the
Karl König Archive...*

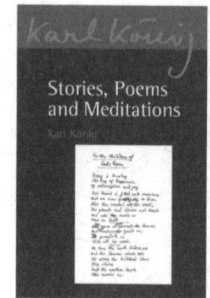

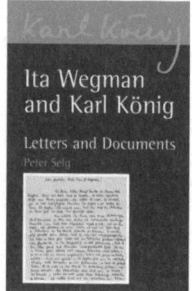

florisbooks.co.uk

Karl König's collected works are being published in English by Floris Books and in German by Verlag Freies Geistesleben. They encompass the entire, wide-ranging literary estate of Karl König, including his books, essays, manuscripts, lectures, diaries, notebooks, his extensive correspondence and his artistic works, across twelve subjects.

Karl König Archive subjects

Medicine and study of the human being
Curative education and social therapy
Psychology and education
Agriculture and science
Social questions
The Camphill movement
Christianity and the festivals
Anthroposophy
Spiritual development
History and biographies
Artistic and literary works
Karl König's biography

Karl König Archive
www.karlkoeniginstitute.org
office@karlkoeniginstitute.org

For news on all our **latest books**, and to receive **exclusive discounts**, **join** our mailing list at:

florisbooks.co.uk

Plus subscribers get a FREE book with every online order!

We will never pass your details to anyone else.